PLAITING
STEP-BY-STEP

PLAITING

STEP-BY-STEP

BY SUELLEN GLASHAUSSER AND CAROL WESTFALL

WATSON-GUPTILL PUBLICATIONS/NEW YORK

Copyright © 1976 by Watson-Guptill Publications

First published 1976 in New York by Watson-Guptill Publications,
a division of Billboard Publications, Inc.,
One Astor Plaza, New York, N.Y. 10036

Library of Congress Cataloging in Publication Data
Glashausser, Suellen.
  Plaiting step-by-step.
  Bibliography: p.
  Includes index.
  1. Basketmaking. 2. Braid. I. Westfall,
Carol, joint author. II. Title.
TT879.B3G56   746.4'1   76-22482
ISBN 0-8230-4020-8

First Printing, 1976

*To my mother, Agatha W. O'Brien and
in memory of my father, William J. O'Brien*

For Camille and Maigann

ACKNOWLEDGMENTS

It is next to impossible to list all the fine people who assisted in the compilation of this book. I would however like to thank Susan Jamart for teaching me how to plait, Jon Westfall for his able assistance in the photographic work, Celia Sonenshein for her patient help in editing, and all the enthusiastic young people at Montclair State College who plaited everything in sight, and then some!

Thanks are also extended to Alice Adams, Joanne Brandford, Lillian Elliott, and Ed Rossbach for giving me a deep appreciation of textiles, to the many excellent libraries and museums of New York City, especially the 42nd Street Library and the Museum of Natural History, and to Charlie for perfect grammar and constant understanding.

CONTENTS

Wallpiece by Warren Seelig, 1975. 6″ (15 cm) wide woven elements are plaited to form this geometrically precise wallpiece.

INTRODUCTION

Plaiting is an exciting new art form, though its origins are ancient. Archeologists working in Stone Age and Swiss Lake dwellings have discovered Neolithic vessels with impressions of diagonal plaiting. There is rich evidence that throughout antiquity diverse peoples have plaited a variety of mats, fans, fabrics, containers, decorations, etc.

At the present time, South and Central American peoples, among others, continue the plaiting tradition. The articles they produce are very similar to the ancient pieces. In this broad area, palm and bamboo, two staple plaiting materials, remain abundant and inexpensive.

A variety of plaited baskets, mats, and small animal figures are imported into the United States. A brief look around your home will frequently reveal a number of plaited items, both handmade and industrially produced. Many braids and decorative edgings used in upholstery are machine plaited. Summer straw hats are frequently plaited to shape or made of long lengths of narrow diagonal plaiting which are sewn together. The more we have researched plaiting and thought about it for this book, the more examples of plaiting we have seen. Caned chairs, for instance, are a form of plaiting. Plastic berry baskets are an industrially produced imitation of hand plaited baskets. The ubiquitous Chinese finger puzzles of our youth are beautiful examples of diagonal plaiting.

It is only recently that contemporary fiber artists have begun to plait. They began with the two most basic plaited shapes—a flat rectangular mat and a square or circular basket. Gradually, new materials and new ways of handling plaiting began to evolve. The excitement of this movement is that it is very much in progress. It is an old technique being re-examined by a new people. We come to the technique with a knowledge of its past use but with none of the religious or cultural restrictions which had previously determined its form. We can take plaiting and use it freely, without restraint, as another method of creating textured surfaces or shapes.

Definitions of plaiting are sometimes very broad. In past literature, various braiding techniques, twining, and sprang have been classified as plaiting. In keeping with contemporary classifications we will consider braiding, twining, and sprang as separate disciplines. The body of work which remains falls into two categories—parallel plaiting and diagonal plaiting. Parallel plaiting interlaces in a manner similar to plain weave. In other words, one set of elements might be considered the warp and the other the weft. All intersections are at right angles. It is diagonal plaiting and its variations which produce distinctly flexible products and the most versatile and exciting forms. Diagonal plaits are generally worked continuously; all elements are active. Each pair of elements

is always at right angles and moves across the surface on a diagonal line.

Plaiting is a technique unlimited in width or dimension. Flat, two dimensional pieces of any size can be plaited as well as three dimensional shapes which utilize the simple plaited basket as the origin of their form. Other non-loom techniques require yarn or yarn-like materials such as rope. Plaiting is unique in requiring flat elements. This opens up a range of materials new to non-loom construction, e.g., strips of plastic, printed fabrics, elastic, and paper. This new range of textile materials is currently providing a great stimulus for expression, new challenges, and new horizons.

The plaited grid itself sets an interesting design problem. Elements appear and disappear at regular or irregular intervals. A strong sense of movement is implied as elements recede and come forward. Color and pattern move around and through a piece in varying ways as the plaiting progresses.

Plaiting is relatively rapid, with the time of completion based on the size of the elements. The number of elements and their individual width determine the scale of a piece. Plaiting is also a very portable technique. Pins and a pair of scissors are the basic equipment requirements.

We will begin with a brief history of plaiting and then proceed with an introduction to the range of materials well suited to the technique. We will give you a complete guide for producing a flat sample, a double layered flat sample, and various open and closed containers. In the last chapter, we will consider with you the multitude of possibilities waiting to be explored. We hope you will then be ready to help shape the future of the plaited form in its modern context.

Plaited Ikat IV *by Joan Sterrenburg. 40" x 70" (101.6 x 177.8 cm). Resist-dyed wools and mohairs were loom-woven into strips and then plaited to form this wallpiece. The artist comments: "Basically these works are a result of my exploration of structures which will allow me to exploit color juxtaposition and interaction. Certainly the degree of contrast/value, hue, warm/cool is a crucial concern. The tension between regularity and eccentricity in patterning has always intrigued and fascinated me. For me these pieces deal with that tension as the resist-dyed areas break up the visual structure established by the plaiting."*

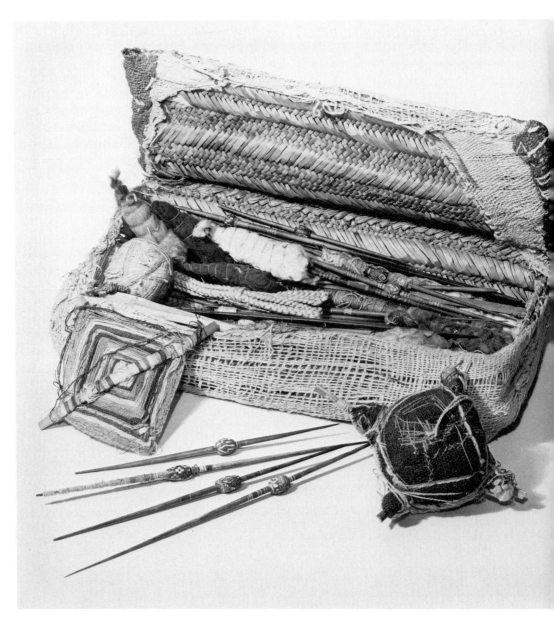

Woman's workbasket, Peru, south coast. 15½″ x 7″ x 3¼″ (39.4 x 17.8 x 8.3 cm). This plaited agave basket dating from the 13th to 15th centuries is covered with cotton cloth. It contains 45 spindles, three weaving swords, seven bobbins of unspun cotton, charms, a braided length of agave, voile carrying cloth, and a ball of thread. Two charms and four spindles are shown in front of the basket. Courtesy of the Newark Museum, Newark, New Jersey.

1

THE HISTORY OF PLAITING

The evolution of plaiting has a long, fascinating history. True perspective on the origins of the technique can be gained from studying its place in primitive cultures. Generally the women plaited, and this activity was as important to the community as cooking and child care. Various plaited containers, bedding, and seating, were major items of home furnishing. Plaited pieces ranged from simply made disposable bowls to elaborate heirloom clothing. These necessities, both fundamental and ornamental, formed the basis of ancient plaiting. We will not attempt to give the definitive history, but we will outline the highlights and give the examples of greatest interest to the contemporary fiber artist.

PLAITING IN ANCIENT TIMES

The available evidence indicates that plaiting, as is the case with other basketry techniques, preceded weaving. Despite the fact that textiles are often destroyed by dampness while buried in the earth, some plaited archeological specimens survive. Several well-preserved pieces can be found in the National Museum of Anthropology in Mexico City. Among these items are three diagonal-plaited sandals from Amasazi, an arid area in northern Mexico. A diagonal-plaited fragment, possibly a mat, still retains a painted geometric design. Most dramatic of all is the mummy of Coixlahuaca from tomb six in Oaxaca. The figure is in a crouching position, surrounded by pottery and completely wrapped in a twill-plaited covering which is anchored by cords. A large, bold, black-and-brown grid is painted on the plaited surface. This particular piece of plaiting is so fine that it is flexible enough to reveal the contours of the body hidden beneath the surface.

Archeologists have found most ancient textile samples in the arid regions of the world. However, many of these pieces have deteriorated into fragments too small to identify. Impressions of plaiting have survived on clay vessels from Stone Age and ancient European sites, but no originals remain. Baking plates from the Michelsberg culture occasionally bear impressions of plaited floor coverings on the sides. These impressions on clay surfaces occur with great frequency on shards from Neolithic times which have been found in the Serbian and southern Hungarian regions.

A woolen fabric with a plaited selvage has come from the Borum Aeshoj (Denmark) finds. This piece dates from the second millennium B.C. Esparto grass plaited fragments dating from the Neolithic cave culture were found at Cueva de los Murcielagos near Albuñol, Spain. Very large plaited containers, possibly granaries, dating from New Kingdom times in Egypt, were discovered embedded in the ground near Mirimde Beni Salame in the Nile Delta. A plaited reedwork basket was unearthed during excavations at Pachacamac, Peru. This particular piece was plaited in a herringbone pattern and dates from the Inca civilization. Other Peruvian plaited pieces were found at Paracas and include a diagonal-plaited workbasket as well as a feather and diagonal-plaited coronet. All of these finds serve to corroborate our belief that plaiting was practiced by primitive peoples throughout the ancient world.

THE AMERICAS

Plaiting in the southwestern United States appears to have had a very long history. Following a beginning foundation period during Basket Maker III times (ca. 400-700 A.D.), excavations have revealed a high development of diagonal-plaited baskets in the Pueblo III (ca. 1000–1300 A.D.) to Pueblo IV (ca. 1300–1700 A.D.) periods. In addition, some of the earliest pottery found in this area bears plaited impressions.

Prehistoric yucca baskets were a typical Cliff Dweller product. Interestingly enough, these old pieces are very similar to contemporary Hopi plaiting in that they utilize the same weave—an over-two, under-two twill, parallel plait. Yucca ring baskets and twill-plaited baskets have been found in the Marsh Pass Cliff Dweller material and at a number of other sites in the area.

The ancient sedentary peoples of the Grand Gulch region in southeastern Utah wore plaited yucca sandals which were worked by beginning at the square toe and proceeding to the heel. Right- and left-footed sandals, plaited to shape at the toes and held by ties onto the foot, have been found at sites in Colorado.

A fragment of ancient pottery from Pope County, Tennessee, bears an impression of plaited basketry with the intriguing combination of a slim and a wide fiber. The plaiting of these two diverse elements was achieved in an over-two, under-two parallel weave.

Another specimen of pre-Columbian diagonal plaitwork was found on the coastline of Louisiana and was given to the Smithsonian Institution in 1866. The preservation of this piece has been attributed to the presence of strong saline soil.

The Brooklyn Museum exhibits a terracotta vase from Honduras dated 800–1200 A.D. This piece bears a perfect trompe l'oeil plaited palm design near the rim.

The history of plaiting is not unlike that of other ancient technologies. As new styles of living and consuming develop, the old ways are forgotten. To a small extent, the historical plaiting we will discuss may continue, but this depends on two factors: the remoteness of the society which supports it and a lack of assimilation into western culture. At the other extreme, the industrialization of a society will, at times, create an atmosphere whereby people can afford to go back to their origins and recreate them or treat them as art forms.

THE PACIFIC

The climate of the Pacific Islands is excellent for both coco palm and pandanus growth. These two plants bear flat leaves which are ideal for plaiting.

The Hawaiian Islands were, in fact, a very important center for plaiting. With few exceptions, the Hawaiians concentrated on making a variety of mats. The coarseness of fineness of both the material and the technique established their use. The pandanus was by far the most important plaiting material until increased cultivation of sugarcane destroyed the pandanus trees. It should be noted that these trees, distinguished by large, straight aerial roots and a crown of narrow leaves, are indigenous to all of the Pacific islands as well as southeastern Asia.

The readily available material stim-

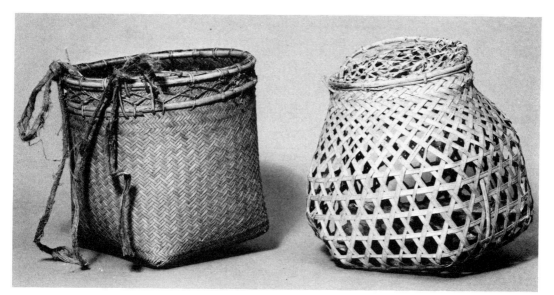

Two baskets from Borneo. The basket on the left is diagonal plaited with a reinforced rim. The basket on the right is open-hexagonal plaited. Courtesy of the American Museum of Natural History.

Plaited house, Nihiru Island, Paumota. Courtesy of the American Museum of Natural History.

Urama taboo-goblin costumes, New Guinea or Papua. Dancers perform around trees and in gardens on which a taboo is to be placed. The taboo ensures adequate food for ceremonial feasts. Courtesy of the American Museum of Natural History.

ulated Hawaiian *nala* (plaiting). Women, the traditional plaiters in Hawaiian society, excelled in creating twill diagonal-plaited sleeping mats made from a sedge called *makaloa* (*Cyperus laevigatus*). These mats could only be made during specific times of the year when there was a new growth of sedge. A unique feature of *makaloa* mats was the *opiki* technique. This was a doubling of the marginal strips on the two side edges and a long twist of the marginal wefts at the upper and lower edges. Coarse mats were subjected to greater wear, so these pieces were double-plaited to give them greater durability.

After the arrival of the missionaries, color was introduced into the plaited surface by overlaying. Red strips, from the sheath at the base of the sedge stem, were used to form motifs on one surface only. For large motifs, a second red strip was laid over the basic strip as the plaiting progressed. For small areas, red strips could be inserted after a mat was complete. Motifs ranged from geometric designs to words and greetings not unlike those used in early American samplers. Tiny Pitcairn Island in the Pacific was peopled by Europeans who plaited quite in keeping with the Pacific tradition and who, like the Hawaiians, also plaited words into the basket and mat fabrics.

It is interesting to note the relationship between the baskets and the mats in the Pacific Islands. (We have also seen this in Central America.) A basket is a folded-up mat and a mat can be a basket opened out flat. Mats are used like baskets to carry or transport things. They are rather like our plastic bags, all-purpose carryalls, except that they can be opened up and used as ground cloths.

Very fine mats are no longer made in Hawaii, but there are 20 beautiful, old examples in the collection of the Bernice P. Bishop Museum in Honolulu. These pieces average about eight feet by ten feet and the finest weave is 25 strips per inch. In this case, the pieces were probably worn as cloaks rather than used as mats.

Sleeping mats were arranged in piles. The coarsest mat lay on the floor, the finest lay on top, and medium-plaited pieces were layered in between. This sandwich was then sewn together at the edges to keep all the mats in place. Floor mats, unlike the sleeping mats, were immense pieces plaited in one large panel. These mats were called *lauhala* and were used especially in the churches, which had no pews.

Rectangular or square pillows (*uluna*) were plaited of pandanus and stuffed with the pandanus leaves. These pieces were usually parallel plaited with overlay designs similar to those used on the sleeping mats. Small cubical pillows were also used as balls in many Pacific Island games.

Hand fans in several distinctive shapes were plaited in Hawaii and throughout Polynesia. Hawaiian coco-leaf fans usually utilized the midrib as a handle. Samoan fans were very airy and delicate in contrast to the coarsely plaited fans of Fiji.

In Puna, Hawaii, the bracts of the male pandanus flowers were used for the most highly prized mats. The naturally short strips were cut into very narrow widths before work began. To the south in Samoa, a lush layer of pile was sometimes added to a mat after it was plaited. One such specimen in the Bishop Museum has a 7 inch long pile, creating a rich vegetal fur surface.

In some Pacific Island areas, such as Samoa, very fine flat-plaited pieces were used as items of apparel. Pandanus was scraped until paper thin and then plaited into 2 or 3 yard pieces as soft and flexible as dress fabric. The edges were fringed and the most beautiful of these pieces were embellished in random areas with small scarlet feathers. Years might be spent in creating an heirloom mat cloth which would be passed on from one generation to the next. These pieces were, of course, worn only on special occasions.

Marshall Islanders used mats as apronlike garments. Sometimes two were worn at once, one in the front and one in the back. They were then tied around the waist apron-style. The other possibility was to wear a single mat which passed between the legs with the ends anchored over a coiled belt. These garment mats were patterned specifically according to rank and sex. For instance, diagonal-plaited loincloths were worn by the men of the Tuamotu Archipelago only, while women wore the magenta-stained plaited aprons of the New Hebrides. These latter apron mats were woven with delicate open weaves which formed chevron and other geometric designs.

Throughout the South Pacific, during pre-European times, plaited mats formed sails on the large ocean-going vessels which traveled among the scattered islands. Two different plaiting methods were employed in the fashioning of these sails. In Tahiti, several large mats were plaited and then sewn together. In the Marshall Islands, a special arched lapboard was used by the sail plaiters as they wove 4 to 7 inch wide plaited strips of pandanus leaves. The strips were overlapped and sewn together with coconut fiber and sharp bone needles. These sails were twice as heavy as an ordinary mat and a little heavier than the canvas we use today. A few strips of dyed hibiscus fiber were overlaid on the diagonal plaiting (over-two, under-two), forming colored lines across the face of the fabric.

The British Museum houses an ancient triangular Maori sail. Double-zigzag colored strips run vertically down the sail, and the top is decorated with feathers. The fabric is made of *kiekie* (flax), and the piece measures 14 feet

long, 6 feet, 4 inches wide at the top and 12 inches at the base.

Plaiting was more diverse in the Philippines. Less emphasis was placed on mats and more attention was paid to specific construction for a particular purpose. The omnipresent pointed Philippino hat (*salacot*) was plaited from bamboo, pandanus, and palm with variations in shape for men and women. Openwork models were often lined with leaves. Twill parallel plaiting called *sawali* was woven and sold in large rolls throughout the Philippines. It was used as a basic construction element for walls, screens, partitions, ceilings, and shutters. Small sections were cut and used as mats to dry fish and rice.

An aboriginal group, the Jacanes, living in the interior of Basilan Island, the Philippines, also plaited. They wove a hexagonal-plaited bolo case which was used to carry tools and equipment and which hung from the waist of the wearer. This sturdy item was created by plaiting an open-hexagonal bamboo base with an outer layer of *anyam gila* (three-strand hexagonal plaiting).

Large-scale twill-checkerwork bamboo plaiting formed the walls of the houses in the Society Islanders. Plaited sandals made from the bark of the purau tree (hibiscus) were worn by the plaiters, and native arrowroot was highly valued as the material to use in plaiting hats.

In most countries, the surface of plaited work is unembellished and prized for its smoothness and sheen; however, witch doctors in Sarawak, Borneo, made use of heavily adorned plaited medicine baskets. One very old diagonal-plaited basket from the Saribas River contains an array of charms. It is wooden and the outside surface is covered with plaited rattan Wooden splints support the outer sides. The strips on the large diagonal-plaited rattan base split to give the

Contemporary knapsack, the Philippines. 15" high, 10" wide (38.1 x 25.4 cm). Wooden supports around the base permit this basket to stand when not in use. Collection of Mr. and Mrs. Barry Boonshaft. Photo by John Carlano.

Contemporary long-handled basket, the Philippines. 11" high (not including handle), 9" at widest diameter (28 x 23 cm).

body a much finer plaited surface. The rim is decorated with dangling braids. Strings crisscross the basket surface, connecting such diverse items (all of a magical nature) as a tuft of dried bamboo leaves, a small skin-covered china pot containing oil, two porcupine quills for dispensing oil, two bear canine teeth, a small horn cylinder, and a small piece of wood wrapped up in cloth. Somewhat similar in feeling is a lavish ceremonial mask from the Sepic River region in New Guinea, although this cone-shaped diagonal-plaited piece dates from the twentieth century. It is an imposing plaited form with a height of about four feet and a spectacular decorated fringe.

Murut basketmakers in Northern Borneo plaited mats, baskets, hats, and other items from rattan, bamboo, bemban, and pandanus. On special occasions, such as feasts, small mats usually one foot by two feet or less were hung on house posts and walls as decorations. The Murut divided bemban stems into strands of four distinct qualities. The glossy outer surface was most highly valued. The inner layers were reserved for plaiting hat linings or for rough mats. Colored strips formed the basis for patterns which, once plaited, told long, complex stories. A plaiter's skill was demonstrated on large parallel- or diagonal-plaited mats with a variety of patterns based on five colors: black, red, white, yellow, and purple. On both mats and baskets, distinct border patterns were utilized to finish off a piece. Designs were formed by individually plaiting colored strips or by superimposing a different color on an already completed solid background. All-white mats with a brocadelike surface were created by alternating the matte side of the plaiting strip with the shiny side.

In New Zealand, emphasis was placed on disposable baskets. The Maori wives made extensive use of plaited bands while preparing food.

Before each meal, a woman quickly plaited green flax into a collar form which was placed around the rim of the umu (earth oven). This plaited collar prevented the food from spilling off the heated rocks. During each use, the plaited collar shrank and became loose, and was later discarded. Plaited receptacles for cooked food and plaited pot covers constituted standard household equipment. Even disposable plaited food bowls were used by Maori families. Equally disposable were the flax or mountain grass (Cordyline australis) sandals woven by the Maori in pre-European times. Examples of these ancient sandals were found in caves in Otago. Plaiting was begun at the big toe and sometimes continued up the leg in a kind of Greco-Roman style. During expeditions in rough, stony country or in swamps, each person carried five to 20 extra pairs of sandals. During rest stops, sandal plaiting from available materials would continue in order to maintain an adequate supply.

ASIA

In Formosa, baskets were the most important domestic utensil. Ten or twelve baskets serving a multitude of differing purposes were standard household equipment. There were diagonal- or parallel-plaited burden baskets, cradles, trays for different foods (special trays were reserved for betel nuts and tobacco), tool baskets, open hexagonal bamboo hats, parallel-plaited winnowing trays, and pot covers. Baby cradles and creels for carrying freshly caught fish were combination-plaited in diagonal and parallel plaiting. The round twill parallel-plaited trays were worked flat with the ends bent back and woven in at the edge. A piece of string was threaded through this edge space and shortened until a shallow tray shape with a distinct rim was formed. A bamboo splint was then stitched onto the rim for reinforcement. Bamboo was used green by the southern peoples, and rattan was the preferred material of the northern groups. Formosa's most dramatic contribution to plaiting was the turtleback-shaped rain protector of the Budai-Rukai. These structures were plaited in an open hexagonal weave and were lined with leaves to make them rainproof. They were worn slung on the shoulders like turtle shells.

Large quantities of bamboo, rattan, vine, and willow together with the native tradition of flower arranging have made a significant impact on Japanese plaiting. Both the open hexagonal and diagonal plaiting were techniques frequently employed. Old, graceful flower baskets are quite unlike the basic round or rectangular baskets of Malaysia or Hawaii. If anything, these

pieces are more like curving, flowing glass vases in form. By varying the width of the plaiting elements, the Japanese plaiters subtly changed the shapes of their baskets. A much-sought-after rich-brown plaiting strip came from bamboo pieces salvaged from old houses, where age and smoke had darkened the wood. The attention to detail in these delicate baskets is extraordinary; they possess a very formal, sophisticated character.

Plaited bamboo baskets were an important part of the sericulture industry. Mulberry leaves were collected in these baskets, and the worms were stored on plaited trays. Flat hexagonal-plaited baskets also served for rearing silkworms in An-Hui province in China.

The firing of tea leaves was conducted in a pinched, cylindrical

Japanese lunch box, antique. 7" x 5" x 3½" (17.8 x 12.7 x 8.9 cm). The twill diagonal-plaited case encloses a three-sectioned metal food container. Bamboo and leather reinforcements, metal fittings, and a tasseled cord contribute to the elegance of this piece. Collection of Mr. and Mrs. Barry Boonshaft. Photo by John Carlano.

Contemporary open hexagonal-plaited Chinese hat. 19½″ diameter (49.5 cm). Leaves line the interior of this piece, forming another pattern under the plaited surface. The beautiful details on the point and around the rim are plaiting variations. Collection of Mr. and Mrs. Barry Boonshaft. Photo by John Carlano.

Shirt of matting, Tanala, Madagascar. This shirt is actually composed of four diagonally plaited sections which have been joined together. Photo courtesy of the Department of Anthropology, National Museum of Natural History, Smithsonian Institution, Cat. No. 1915A.

plaited bamboo basket called *take-hoiro*. A small hibachi rested in the lower section of the basket, and a plaited bamboo tray rested on pegs over the fuel. The tea leaves were arranged on this tray.

As late as 1925, farmers near Peking, China, were burying an oval-plaited willow-twig basket with the dead. In life this basket served as a grain measure, but in death the wooden hoop reinforcing the rim was removed and food was heaped in the basket.

It was not unusual for old Chinese baskets to be lacquered in red and gold, adding to their already stiff, formal elegance. Open hexagonal plaiting was triple-layered to give a very complex textured surface which still retained a light quality. This technique of layering was sometimes implemented by using wide, light elements to form the innermost layer, medium-width brown strips to form the middle layer, and fine, light strips for the outermost layer. The resulting surface was called grape design. Due to the scale changes, each layer contributed visually to the complete basket. Many layers of open hexagonal plaiting gave great depth and beauty to the surface of the old carrying baskets.

Ornate baskets were often partly wooden, fitted with elaborate metal trim and locks and graced with carved wooden handles. Long messages were plaited into these very delicately made baskets. One reads, "May your hall be filled with happiness and prosperity." The character "fu," for good luck, was plaited into the baskets used to carry the books and papers of candidates who were traveling to the capital to take the civil service exams.

In Tongin, Vietnam, the people once crossed rivers in twill-plaited boats. Wide strips of bamboo were parallel-plaited into an egglike shape measuring about 12½ feet long, 5 feet wide, and 26 inches deep. A mixture of cow dung and coconut oil was periodically

daubed on the interstices to keep the craft watertight.

AFRICA

The origins of the plaiting technique are uncertain, but some scholars feel that plaiting was brought to Africa by Arabs from the east. The most elaborate mats, which are plaited on the east-coast islands, lend substance to this theory. Pandanus was the material used for the large parallel-plaited mats. Various twill patterns were superbly utilized in order to produce the most intricate designs. Over-four, under-one twill weave is the most common pattern, but the scope of the plaiting ranges from over-one, under-one to over-six, under-six. Red strips were worked in with the natural colored elements. Africans made this technique appear very similar to tapestry by plaiting animals and human figures in many different positions and also by utilizing asymmetrical abstract designs. In Madagascar, sedge was diagonal-plaited into shirts and curly-topped hats.

EUROPE

The small amount of information available to us on European plaiting leads to the impression that it was a much less important part of life than in the previously discussed areas. However, archeological finds we have mentioned indicate that plaiting was practiced by the ancient European tribes. In more recent times, straw diagonal-plaited bags with leather appliqués were made in Czechoslovakia. Similar diagonal-plaited containers, decorated with leather, were made in Nieder-bayern, Germany, in the early 1800s. During this same period, the Italian straw hat industry was an important one, and plaited hats were produced by sewing long, narrow plaited strips together.

INDIAN PLAITING

As noted earlier, American and Canadian Indian sites reveal plaiting to be of very ancient origin. A variety of basketry styles and types exists across the country. The available material seems to dictate the particular basket construction. In general, the natural elements at hand were better suited to the coiling and twining techniques. Groups of Indians on the northwest coast and in the southeast plaited extensively, and there appear to be other widely separated areas where the plaiting technique was employed. The availability of leaves from the yucca plant in the southwest, for instance, stimulated the use of plaiting in that area.

Cedar bark was an important raw material on the northwest coast and was used for both parallel and diagonal plaiting. Cedar-bark ribbons are a rich, dark color, and their softness distinguishes them from all other plaiting materials. These ribbons make a soft, baglike fabric rather than a stiff basket. Mats of cedar bark were placed on floors and used as mattresses, tablecloths, and upholstery. Guests at the recurring ceremonial potlatch feasts sat on parallel-plaited cedar-bark mats, which were later given away.

The Nootka plaited pouches or envelope shapes without bases. Fantastic parallel-plaited raincoats and large-brimmed hats came from the Kwakiutl, who also made use of diagonal- and parallel-plaited mats as ceremonial food servers for adolescent girls. The Haida, Challam, and Tsimshian plaited large bags, some with drawstrings at the top. The Bella Coola, as with other tribes in cold areas, produced diagonal-plaited snowshoes.

The Haida worked black-and-brown cedar-bark mats with parallel and twill parallel plaiting in the same piece. Beautiful surfaces resulted from these slight changes in technique. Another Haida variation was to use four rows of parallel plaiting, one row of diagonal plaiting, four rows of parallel plaiting, etc.

In the southeast, baskets were plaited of split wild cane, a glossy material which took dyes well. Red and dark brown were favored colors. Canebreaks grew throughout the southeastern lowlands in North Carolina, South Carolina, Georgia, Florida, Alabama, Mississippi, and Louisiana. The Cherokee, Choctaw, Creek, Chickasaw, Seminole, Attakapa, Alibamu, and Chitimacha tribes plaited stiff, lidded baskets with geometric patterns inspired by nature, e.g., alligator intestines, worm tracks, cattle eyes, and blackbird eyes. The Creek and Chitimacha twisted the ends into an imitation braid at the rim. This plaiting is very similar to that of mats found in caves in Kentucky and to Yaqui work in Mexico.

The plaiter split the cane with his or her teeth and then dyed the split strands red, black, or yellow. In order to achieve a glossy interior as well as exterior, the cane was double-plaited with the inner woody surfaces together. Chitimacha baskets were always oblong and ranged from one inch to one foot in height. An important element in Chitimacha life, these baskets served as containers for the storage of food and as urns for the ashes of the deceased.

The Choctaw plaited a basket form somewhat like an inverted triangle. It served as a box for presenting gifts and was considered an imitation of a heart. They also made an elbow-shaped basket with a handle, cow-nose baskets, and wall pockets. If cane was not available, stems from the sabal palmetto were used. This plant is actually a small palm tree with fan-shaped leaves. In the southeast, it is commonly referred to as cabbage palmetto.

The Iroquois League of Six Na-

Antique domed basket, India. 18″ high, 15″ at the widest diameter (45.7 x 38.1 cm). Variations of twill patterning break up the surface into small units. Collection of Mr. and Mrs. Barry Boonshaft. Photo by John Carlano.

Chafing basket, Amazon. The white zigzag lines are a powdery pigment applied after completion of the basket. Collection of Debra Shatin.

Eva Wolfe, contemporary Cherokee basketmaker from North Carolina, plaiting a river-cane basket. Courtesy of the Indian Arts and Crafts Board, United States Department of the Interior.

tions—the Mohawk, Oneida, Onondaga, Cayuga, Seneca, and Tuscarora—were the most active splint basketmakers. They soaked and pounded logs until each annual layer peeled off easily. These were then split with a basket gauge to produce the splints. An interesting rim treatment was to sandwich the ends between two splints to form a double hoop and a very strong edge. This was a variation employed by the Iroquois, who also sewed together flat diagonal-plaited strips to make shoes. Open hexagonal-plaited hominy sieves are yet another Iroquois invention. The Cayuga are known for their parallel-plaited dart holders.

The Algonquin tribes in New England usually parallel-plaited splint baskets. However, diagonal plaiting was sometimes employed, especially in the production of snowshoes. Diagonal-plaited cedar-bark bags were used for storing wild rice. We were delighted to come upon one old Mohican basket which had potato-printed designs stamped on the elements.

The Penobscot in Maine plaited an open-hexagonal-weave colander which could be the precursor of our modern metal colander. The Niantic of Connecticut used an open-hexagonal-weave basket for rinsing clothes.

The Arikara of Dakota, the Hidatsa, Mandan, Cherokee, and Catawba, who lived along the upper Missouri River, plaited splint pack baskets with U-shaped rod corners. Vegetables were sometimes collected in these containers. Mandan gambling bowls from the central plains were diagonal-plaited and reinforced with wooden ribs at each corner. Plaiting also existed to a certain extent among the Great Lakes Indians and the Southern Plains groups.

Hopi yucca plaiting was the most prominent in the Southwest. The Jemez, most noted of the Hopi plaiters, created mats, baskets, headrings, pottery rests, and cradle hoods.

The Pima, who lived in the southern California desert area, used agave leaves to diagonal-plait. The Papago in Arizona also used the diagonal-plaiting technique in their basketry.

Diagonal plaiting has been employed over a long period of time in Mexico, Central America, Guiana, Peru, and Ecuador. Yucca and palm are easily accessible raw materials in these areas and thus stimulated the use of the technique. In Mexico, cylindrical double-weave covered baskets were made by the Tarahumara. These particular baskets are very similar to the canework of the Chitimacha. The Yaqui and Huichol in northern Mexico and the Otomi in central Mexico all produced quantities of diagonal-plaited baskets and mats.

A diagonal-plaited hat has been excavated from the central coast of Peru. It is a most interesting design, having open spaces alternating with closed areas and tabs which extend in a vertical line down each side. Forest tribes from the interior created diagonal-plaited pieces which were lavishly embellished with feathers. Other tribes hexagonal-plaited and diagonal-plaited fans, small cases, and parallel-plaited blow-gun covers.

The Indians of Mexico, Central America, North and South America, and the Caribbean Islands used a manioc (cassava) press to remove poison (hydrocyanic acid) from the manioc root. This root was processed to make manioc flour, a substance similar to tapioca. The press was in use as early as 892 A.D. and is still a household item in some areas. It is a long, slender, diagonal-plaited basket with a handle-type loop at one end. The manioc is pounded and forced into the press until the mass becomes half as short and twice as wide as it was in the original state. The press is then submerged in water and left to soak. It is next hung by the loop from an available branch with a weight attached to the opposite closed end. The weight stimulates the squeezing action which drains away the poison and brings the press back to its original long, narrow shape. The entire process must be repeated several times before the manioc is ready for use.

The Cayapa Indians of Ecuador plaited with two, three, and four elements. They culled plaiting materials from five different plants. One plant, an aerial root used for heavy work, was 75 to 100 feet long. Plaited items included mats, rests for calabashes, baskets to hold spindles, and square-shaped twill (over-three, under-three) parallel-plaited fire fans. Some baskets were woven with drawstrings at the rim. The three- and four-element plaiting was all open hexagonal and complex variations of this weave. Three-element open-hexagonal plaiting was considered to resemble a human eye.

The Arawak Indians of British Guiana, now Guyana, lived on land drained by both the Pomeroon and Moruca Rivers. They worked with three basic plaiting materials: palm (*Astrocaryyum tucumoides*), aerial stems (*Carludovica plumierii*) and reed *(Phragmites* and *Arundo).* The latter was well suited for the creation of cassava presses, sifters, and baskets. The men of the tribes plaited, using an over-three, under-three diagonal plait for the cassava presses, some of which measured over 6 feet in length. Strands to be used for the handle were left unplaited and were woven only when the piece was completed. Fan handles were completed in a similar manner. Open-hexagonal- and diagonal-plaited knapsacks were made in two types; one for permanent use and the other to be disposed of after one usage. The Arawak conical basket is similar to the Choctaw heart basket by virtue of its shaping. The sides of these hourglass-shaped baskets are a series of curves, all controlled by the closeness or open areas of the diagonal plaiting. An

open-hexagonal-weave conical fish catcher and, on a larger scale, the thatched roofs of the Arawak dwellings were also plaited by these peoples.

Beautiful fantasy containers were diagonal-plaited in the Dutch West Indies (the Netherlands Antilles). This area was also one of the few centers for *anyam gila* (three-strand hexagonal plaiting), the most complicated of the plaiting techniques, which means, in a literal sense, "mad chicken." Open-hexagonal plaiting is as airy as its name implies and quite easy to master, but it should not be confused with the solid, three-strand surface of the true *anyam gila*. Certain areas of Indonesia, the Philippines, and the Marshall Islands in Micronesia, as well as the Dutch West Indies, were the exclusive centers of *anyam gila* plaiting.

Pandanus (*Pandanus fascicularis*), commonly called screw pine, was the material used for *anyam gila* in Tanjong Kling, Malacca. After a laborious preparation by old women, baskets were started with a star of six narrow strands called the navel of the Belanek fish. Additional strands were woven in, two at a time, at each corner. Upon reaching the desired size, a length of split rattan was inserted to reinforce the turn and the sides were plaited, completely covering the rattan. *Anyam gila* was plaited with single-ply strips from the center of the base to the rim, then the strips were interplaited backwards to the center of the base. In the process of doubling the plaiting, the strips were twisted and turned to make patterns called rice grains.

Hexagonal-plaited baskets were usually produced in nests of five, with two strands added to each progressively larger piece. Many of the women could plait only the *anyam gila* basket style, and few of the plaiters were able to create oval, triangular, or diamond shapes. Actually, the rectangular and square baskets which were woven are

Contemporary diagonal-plaited
baskets, Mexico. 10″ high, 9″
diameter (25.4 x 22.9 cm).

Chitimacha heart basket. Courtesy of the American Museum of
Natural History.

Contemporary diagonal-plaited basket, Colombia. 14½″ high (not including handle), 10″ wide (36.8 x 25.4 cm). The elements are tightly plaited at both the rim and base and are allowed to spread apart for the main open work area. Courtesy of the Gallery Shop, Brooklyn Museum. Photo by John Carlano.

by far the most difficult to accomplish. Three to four months of daily work were necessary to complete a fine nest. Female prisoners in the jails of Singapore were taught to plait the *anyam gila* weave and were then required to produce the difficult designs. Stepped hexagonal baskets were developed in tiers with the lid of one basket forming the base of the next. A few rare *anyam gila* baskets were plaited with pointed covers. While these baskets are technically the most difficult to achieve, they are not necessarily more beautiful than some of the other pieces we have discussed.

PLAITING TODAY

Plaiting exists today but in a far different context. As technology advances, baskets become less a necessity and more a tourist attraction or a cheap export to the industrialized countries. If the raw material is no longer free and abundant, or even available, then basketry is threatened. Of course this is not always true and depends very much on the situation in a particular area. In general, the less complex forms still exist but there is a watering down of the old traditions.

Plaited ceilings, screens, large-scale fences, and simple baskets are still very evident in Japan. Small, fragile plaited toys remain inexpensive but must compete with bright plastic models. Parallel-plaited baskets, similar to the work of the Hopi, continue to be available in the Japanese countryside. Flower arranging remains an important aspect of life, so flower baskets of elaborate delicacy continue to be plaited for formal, semiformal, and informal arrangements. An incredible attention to detail is evident in these new baskets. Open-hexagonal-weave hats are still plaited in a variety of shapes and lined with leaves not only in Japan but in China as well. Information on Chinese plaiting is scant, but from the baskets we have seen, we must assume that the plaiting technique is very much in use in that vast country.

In Africa, there is also a living tradition of plaiting. Plaited mats and baskets are often seen in the background of pictures of items such as sculpture and masks. Sixty mat patterns have been collected in Zanzibar, all named after designs occurring in nature. These mats are very rich, in both the variety of their execution and their conception. They are plaited in strips of 50 strands each and then the strips are sewn together.

Baskets from the Congo combine techniques in a decorative yet very strong manner. Striking shapes, changing patterns, and bands of cane or sewn edges are characteristic. In Uganda, basketry is very highly developed and is practiced by both men and women. Aside from baskets for everyday use, stockades, fences, huts, and shields are plaited.

The Inter-Lacustrine Bantu parallel-plait baskets in Kiga and Hutu. The Lugbara, Madi, Alur, and Kakwa plait twill-patterned trays. The Ganda, Soga, Gwere, Saniia, Gwe, Teso, Karamoja, and Copi continue to use hexagonal plaiting, as do the Congo Bantu in Amba and Konjo. Wild date palm (*Phoenix reclinata*) or dum palm (*Hyphaens coriacea*) are standard mat materials. The plaited mats are all-purpose; they are bedding, screens, wrappings for possessions, grain-drying mats, and food servers. Tusi and Hima girls cover their heads with mats when traveling beyond their *kraals* (villages). Wives of Nubian soldiers from the Sudan double-plait with two colors. As they work back and forth on a mat, the change in color appears at the edge as they turn the material.

In Chad, open-weave diagonal-plaited fish traps are woven of durable leather strips. The Mbuti pygmies, forest dwellers, also make open-hexagonal-plaited baskets. The Zulu

African nest of baskets. Eleven baskets, reinforced with leather rims and trim, are plaited so as to fit one into another. 9½" high, 6" at widest diameter, 1" at smallest diameter (24.1 x 15.2 x 2.5 cm). These basket nests are reputed to be woven by young girls when they reach the age of puberty, indicating their readiness for marriage. Collection of Carol Westfall. Photo by Jon Westfall.

Two cassava presses, Brazil. (Top) 22" long, 1" diameter (55.9 x 2.5 cm). (Bottom) 24½" long, 2" diameter (62.2 x 5.1 cm). Two contemporary cassava presses from Brazil. The diagonal plaiting creates a very elastic container which is used to remove the poison from the manioc root.

use diagonal-plaited beer strainers; the Lozi parallel-plait flat, traylike baskets; and the Kwele use twill parallel-plaited fishing baskets and huge open-hexagonal plaited baskets for transporting peanuts.

In contrast, it appears that little European plaiting continues today. Some birch-bark plaiting is found in Finland, Norway, and Sweden. In fact, we found a most beautiful example of crude diagonally plaited birch-bark shoes from Finland during our research.

In the United States, plaiting is done on a reduced scale. The Hopi continue to make their traditional circular basket with concentric diamond patterns which they sell to tourists. Fresh green yucca leaves form the twill design against a background of bleached leaves. This basket is plaited flat and then lashed to a rim. It was originally used for winnowing beans.

A handful of Chitimacha, Choctaw, and Cherokee women, all born in the 1920s, have continued cane plaiting. Lela Solomon, a member of the Eastern Band of Choctaw Indians, describes basketmaking during her childhood as a family project. During the winter, every member of the family made baskets, enough to fill a wagon. In the summer, the wagonload of baskets was sold and traded for food and clothing.

Helen Smith, an Eastern Band Cherokee, learned to plait from her mother. They used white oak since the traditional river cane was becoming scarce. Today she also plaits with honeysuckle vines. Mrs. Smith selects natural dyes because they do not fade or run when a basket is washed. She relies on butternut root for black, black walnut root for brown, bloodroot for orange, and yellow root for yellow.

When Rowena Bradley, also a Cherokee, was taught plaiting by her mother, there was only one other person she knew who could make double-cane baskets. She fears that in another generation or two basketmaking will have died out completely among the Cherokee.

A strong plaiting tradition continues in Mexico and throughout Central and portions of South America. The Mexican plaiters cater to the tourists with small plaited animals and baskets, but they use different criteria for the plaited items they make for their own use.

In many shops in the United States we have found baskets, hats, fans, and mats imported primarily from Central and South America, the Philippines, China, and India. These pieces are a mixture of authentic items, i.e., formerly a useful part or still part of a culture, or they are strictly tourist pieces. With increasing assimilation to western ways of thinking, they are becoming more standardized and further removed from being part of the cultures in which they originated. Perhaps a market of selective, informed buyers will provide the opportunity for the old examples to continue, if no longer for practical or ceremonial use, then as baskets of great dignity and extraordinary beauty, prized as objets d'art.

Plaited ties by Bonnie Scrimgeour. 12″ high, 6″ diameter at the base (30.5 x 15.2 cm). An enclosed, stuffed shape is formed by plaiting mens' ties with the wide ends used to form the base.

2

TOOLS AND MATERIALS

Ribbonlike strips of fiber or fabric, either natural or synthetic, are the elements indigenous to most plaiting. We have found it very stimulating to search out new and nontraditional supplies that are flat and therefore uniquely suited for use with this technique.

Historically, preparation of the raw material has ranged from merely cutting leaves from trees and plants to very elaborate, ritualized conditioning of the fiber. Some baskets are only used once and these are quickly made from available leaves. On the other hand, Panama hats and other very finely plaited objects require materials which have been carefully grown, selected, and processed.

The necessary equipment for plaiting will vary with the amount of preparation your selected material requires. A very special basket or mat may necessitate long and careful preparation of the elements as well as an array of diverse tools. The particular material determines exactly what implements and procedures are necccssary to create the desired shape or form.

We will first review some traditional materials and the tools and steps required for their preparation. These techniques are usually handed down from one generation to another and reflect a close relationship among method, material, and finished product.

WOOD

In the United States, the Seneca make splint baskets from wood. This basically resistant material requires the maximum of equipment. The Seneca women use an axe, a straight-bladed jackknife which is not too sharp, a basket gauge (a small tool with up to nine parallel blades which will cut one piece of splint into ten narrow, even strips), a screwdriver, and a piece of thick cloth which is used to protect the plaiter's knees while the splints are being cut.

PALM

So-called Panama hats are actually produced in several countries in Central America as well as in Ecuador and Colombia. They are made from strips of palm (*Carludovica palmata*) which are processed until they become extremely pliant. The plant is cut just before ripening. The leaves are boiled, sun-dried, and sorted. Next, the material is dampened and divided into the required widths with the thumbnail. Individual strands of this material are so fine and fragile that they must be plaited from midnight to seven A.M. only, when the air is most humid. A fine hat is the result of three to five months of nightly labor. When the plaiting is completed, the hat is washed in clean, cold water, coated with a thin solution of gum, and polished with dry, powdered sulphur. The hat is pliable enough to be rolled up in a pocket but very durable, and will last for years.

BAMBOO

Bamboo hats, similar to Panama hats and just as durable, are made in Java. First the bamboo stalks must be cut at the nodes; then these sections are split. The outer skin is removed and the split sections are exposed overnight to the damp air on the basketmaker's roof. The next day, each length is divided into 1¼ inch wide strips. Each of these strips is further split into eight to ten delicate strips. After another exposure to the damp night air, the strips are ready for plaiting.

The tedious preparation for bamboo work is carried on in only three districts in Tahiti. The work must be started in May, June, and July when the shoots are new. The hard green stalks are eventually transformed into rolls of white, satiny, paper-thin plaiting material which is sold in local stores.

The carefully selected center sections of shoots are laid in the shade to season for four days. On the fifth day, the bamboo is cut into sections at the nodes. The thin outer green skin is removed with a penknife. The stalks are then split lengthwise and left in the shade to open naturally and become flat. The strips are now 4½ to 5 inches wide. Several layers are peeled from each section or "pona." These layers are laid flat and weighted with stones in wooden troughs of clear water. The water is changed morning and night. Then the strips are scraped thoroughly with a knife on a smooth, absorbent wooden board reserved for that purpose. The finished pieces are soaked overnight in a trough of water. The next morning, the bleaching process begins. The strips are immersed in a lime juice and water bath for two days. Then a second short scraping removes the last traces of greenish tint. After another soaking in a weaker lime and water solution, the flat strips are dried by scraping them with the dull edge of a knife. The strips are then rolled into large cylinders and are ready for use.

PANDANUS LEAVES

Hawaiian plaiting is principally confined to mat-making, with the pandanus leaf as the major material. All the pandanus leaves are used. The wide, unopened leaves at the center of the cluster make the finest mats, while the lower, dried leaves make coarse, quickly plaited mats. In order to lighten the leaves and make them more pliable, they are smoked in shallow pits. A bed of small pieces of dry wood forms the bottom layer in a pit and creates a hot, smoky, blazeless fire. Green pandanus wood forms the second layer. The green leaves are placed on top of this second layer until they wilt, lose their green color, and become pale. The next step is to draw each leaf through a piece of leaf butt to remove butt and tip ends as well as thorns. Finally, the leaves are sun dried. Rolls of leaves a foot or more in diameter are made in the dampness of evening or on rainy days. Before plaiting, the leaves are beaten and split with a pointed piece of wood or bone.

COCONUT LEAVES

In contrast to this careful preparation, the Hawaiian coconut-leaf basket is discarded after just one usage. Therefore no time at all is spent in preparing the elements. A suitable section of the midrib is cut from a 10 to 12 foot coco-palm leaf and the leaflets are plaited around whatever the contents of the basket will be. The midrib then becomes the handle of the basket and is broken when the contents are removed.

Coconut leaves are given a glossy,

Pacific Island materials. A roll of pandanus, used extensively in Pacific plaiting, can be purchased in the coil form shown in the photograph. The silky, white fiber is hau (hibiscus) and is used for very fine, delicate plaiting. The braided fiber is coconut which we have used to make the lidded basket in Chapter 4. Photo by Jon Westfall.

leatherlike look on the island of Maupiti in the Society Islands. They are dragged slowly across a blazing fire which scorches and toughens them. Sometimes the edges of the leaflets are stripped away, giving a further finish to the material.

NATURAL MATERIALS

The following natural materials are used for plaiting by peoples throughout the world:

agave leaves	yucca leaves
bamboo	coconut leaves
pandanus leaves	palm leaves
reeds	leather
cane	oak splints
hibiscus bark	bulrush
sedge	cedar bark
birchbark	arrowroot
aerial roots	flax
straw	mulberry roots
wild ginger	wide grasses
stems	cattail

These materials are available in widely separated areas of the world. A semitropical or tropical climate is excellent for natural plaiting supplies, although reeds, barks, grasses, and leather are generally fairly abundant in many parts of the more temperate zones. If natural materials are used, it is almost always essential to soak them overnight and to keep them moistened during plaiting. The degree of preliminary flattening and splitting required depends on the delicate quality one wishes to achieve in the finished product.

SYNTHETIC MATERIALS

For the examples in this book, we have utilized the materials natural to our urban culture and, therefore, abundantly available to us. The following is a partial list of some of these manmade materials:

magazines	newspapers
oak tag paper	computer cards
soft cigarette packages	flat elastic
plastic strips	cloth strips
fur strips	ribbon
canvas strips	magnetic tape
cotton webbing	mylar strips
bias tape	zippers
card-woven bands	inkle-woven bands
foam-rubber strips	plastic bags
	metal strips
	wall-paper strips

As with traditional basketry, the finished product is to a great extent dependent on the quality of the material and the amount of time spent in its preparation. Magazine and newspaper strips must be folded to insure sufficient body and pliancy for plaitwork. On the other hand, oak tag paper may be used to good advantage unfolded. Special shapes can result from materials like computer cards because they will hold a crease. Thin cloth strips are best folded in layers, whereas corduroy and felt tend to work well as a single layer.

Any product which can be cut into fairly flexible strips can be plaited. Obviously, a newspaper basket will have a soft, light feel while metal strips will be heavy and more rigid in their shaping possibilities.

Magnetic tape is thin and slippery, therefore difficult to work with. However, the final appearance of a piece plaited with this tape is much more delicate than a piece plaited with cotton webbing. Magnetic tape tends to slip, whereas plastic sticks. Both qualities can be advantageous if used in the right piece.

All types of bands can introduce the excitement of color and patterns within a pattern. In fact, we have found the use of different colored elements to be one of the most fascinating aspects of the plaited form.

Other qualities to consider in a potential material are length, edges, and joining possibilities. Very short strips require many joins during the plaiting process. These joins can be utilized as a design element. Both ragged and straight edges are possible, as well as any combination of the two.

New supplies can be a most stimulating source of inspiration, hence we encourage you to be open to the discovery of new plaiting materials and to the challenge they will offer.

OTHER EQUIPMENT

The equipment you will need is minimal. In working with contemporary materials we have used the following:

straight pins	paper clips
scissors	glovers' needles
yardstick	thread
household	felt-tip pen
dyes	polyester
leather glue	stuffing
tweezers	masking tape

These items are not all necessary for each piece; in fact, a straight edge, scissors, and straight pins are really the only basic equipment requirements. A flat worktable is very helpful at the start, but a dedicated plaiter can work anywhere!

Urban materials. A large pile of dyed zippers forms the background. Two large rolls of continuous beige zippers were found by the authors in a junk antique shop. Each roll was overdyed and will make excellent plaiting material because of the strength and pliancy of the metallic zippers. In the foreground from left to right are a stack of ribbons (some have been resist dyed), rolls of double-plaited wire used on ships, a roll of industrial elastic, and stacks of bright orange, pink, and black plastic.

Chapter I (B) by Debra Rapoport. 27" x 39" (68.6 x 99.1 cm). Old, discarded office tape is the material in this double-faced piece which utilizes both parallel and diagonal plaiting techniques. Bright tassels and wrapped areas highlight one side; the other surface is monochromatic and accented with shiny curls of tape which are clumped together.

(Above) Plaited elastic by Suellen Glashausser. 4 feet x 3 feet (1.2 x .9 m). Hexagonal, diagonal, and parallel plaited white elastic strips have been dyed and crayoned. Joins are sewn. A light stuffing of plastic bags allows the piece to change shape.

(Left) Embellished newspaper cubes by Suellen Glashausser. Individual, hollow plaited cubes are clustered together. Net fruit bags, cut into strips, form an overlay layer. Fruit decals, ribbon, and fake flowers obscure some of the printing. Decorated ends protrude into space and, on the far left, one cube has a plastic foam extension. Photos by John Carlano.

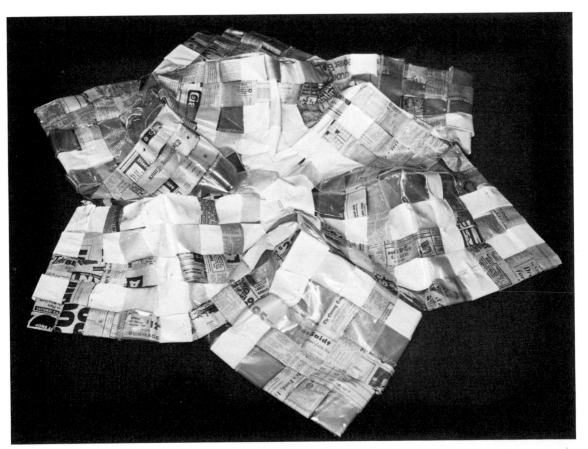

(Above) Newspaper and plastic plaiting by Marla Acaster. 4 feet x 4 feet (1.2 x 1.2 m). Zigzag, machine-stitched plastic strips (both clear and opaque) are diagonal plaited with newspaper. Straight pins and paper clips remain. This piece was inspired by a traditional Indian basket base with a six-strand start and additional elements added along the ribs as the plaiting progressed.

(Right) Plaited handbag by Angus Dupree. 10″ x 7″ x 3½″ (25.4 x 17.8 x 8.9 cm)—not including handle. Prisoners in the Rahway State Prison, Rahway, New Jersey, plait empty cigarette packages into bags, picture frames, wallets, etc. Four hundred packages are necessary to complete one handbag. The cellophane is kept on each strip and every square is the visible portion of one cigarette package, making the pieces very solid and durable. In fact, although the technique looks exactly like diagonal plaiting, it is actually a variation which is worked in long chains. Once these zigzag chains are complete, they are tied together with the handle as a separate chain.

Señora Serafin Fuentes plaiting a basket in her shop in Oaxaca, Mexico. Señora Fuentes specializes in plaiting soft, supple basket forms which can be folded flat.

3

THE FLAT PLAITED FORM

Flat plaiting refers to the creation of either single- or double-layered two-dimensional surfaces. These pieces may be shaped symmetrically or unsymmetrically.

The *petates* (mats) woven in Michoacán, Mexico, are perfect examples of the use man has made, and continues to make, of this technique. The mat is plaited of flattened reeds in a combination two-over-two and one-over-three weave, creating a single-layer surface. The firm, yet supple quality inherent in the flattened stalks creates a most comfortable mat which is a staple item in the homes of the poor. The mats are used to cover doorways, to sit on, to eat on, to sleep on; in other words, they are an everyday necessity and are used in a variety of ways.

Double plaiting has historically been used either to add extra strength to an item or to create containerlike pieces. The contemporary double-plaited bag made in the Philippines as well as the money belt and the change purse from Oaxaca, Mexico aptly illustrate this point. In the directions which follow, we will be using the double-layered technique to create a stuffed pillow form.

As you plait, it will become obvious that you can easily control the width and length of the piece by simply adding or deleting bands. The creation of corners at different sections enables you to alter the shape of the piece. We have also found that by preplaiting a sampler in newspaper strips and using magic markers to denote color, we have been able to work out some interesting variations on the technique. Using newspaper also enables you to premeasure, so that when you buy selected materials, you know exactly how much is necessary for any given project.

In the following pages we will take you through the steps necessary to plait a single-layer and a double-layer mat in newspaper. Then we will give you directions for making a single-layer "bird," "rocket," or "sputnik" shape. (We decided it has many different interpretations!) This particular piece will teach you how to shape the plaiting to create corners. We chose cotton canvas webbing as this material is easily dyed and is washable. The shape lends itself to use as a placemat for a child, a wallhanging, or, if hung in space, a mobile.

The double-layer sampler is, as we mentioned, stuffed to form a pillow. This piece is made of washable goatskin suede strips and is stuffed with polyester fibers.

Let's plait.

This sampler will enable you to begin plaiting in the simplest form possible. We will use newspaper as it is readily available and is a pliant, sturdy plaiting material.

To complete the sampler, you will need one page of standard-size newspaper, i.e., one-half of a whole sheet, straight pins, a black felt-tip pen or magic marker and, if you wish, a pair of scissors. (We prefer to prefold the newspaper and simply tear the strips along the fold lines.) The straight pins are used, as needed, to secure corners, etc., as you work.

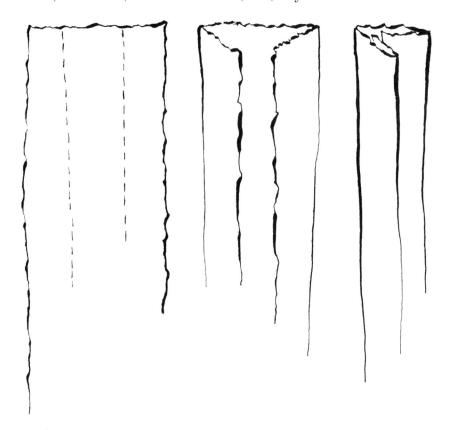

Take one standard-size sheet of newspaper and tear or cut it along the centerfold. Take one page and fold it evenly into four lengthwise sections. Tear or cut the paper along the fold lines so you have four strips (A) and fold it into a 1″ wide band as shown above, first folding the raw edges towards the center (B), then folding in half (C). The raw edges are now enclosed within the band. Do the same to the other three strips. Now, with a black felt-tip pen, color two of the bands black, both front and back. (Note that in the following directions, we refer to the plain newspaper bands as the "white" bands.)

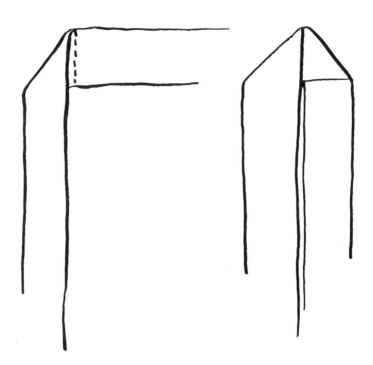

Fold one of the white bands in half lengthwise (A). Proceed to fold a 45° angle along the fold line (B). Then, fold the right side back *under* itself on a 45° angle (C). This forms the first corner.

Fold a black band in half to create a line marking the center of the band. Plait (one-under, one-over), and center the fold mark of the black band in between the two vertical strips of the white band (A and B). Now fold both the left and the right sides of the black band over at 45° angles (C). Note that the left side folds *over* on top of itself, and that the right side folds *under* itself.

Fold the third band (white) in half and plait it in, making
certain to center the strip. Again, fold both the left and
the right sides of the band over at 45° angles.

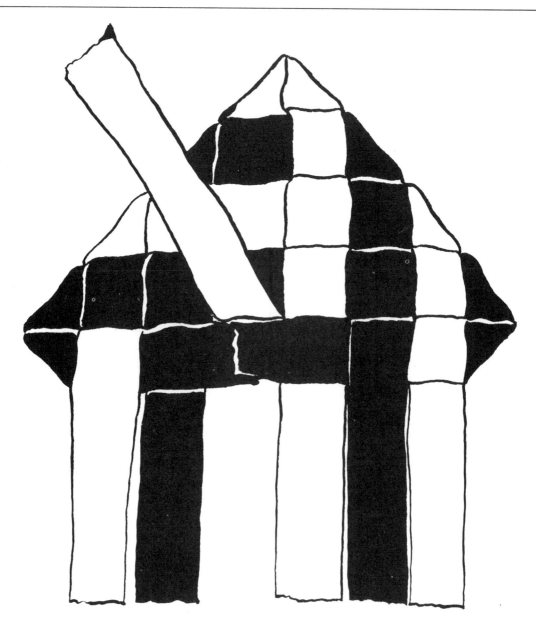

Fold the fourth band (black) in half and plait it in (under and over each of the vertical elements). Turn each side at 45° angles; the right side *under* itself and the left side *over* itself. Now repeat this same fold so the left side folds *over* itself a second time and is plaited back into the piece. The right side is turned *under* itself and plaits in to merge with the band coming from the left side. The two bands in combination then form the fifth line of weaving. (Cut off the ends of these strips so each end is neatly concealed under one of the covering or vertical strips).

Take the left band and fold it *over* itself on a 45° angle and plait it in until it ends. Fold the right band *under* itself on a 45° angle and plait it in to merge with the band coming from the left. Again, cut away any excess horizontal bands so the ends overlap and stop under a vertical band (see Step 5).

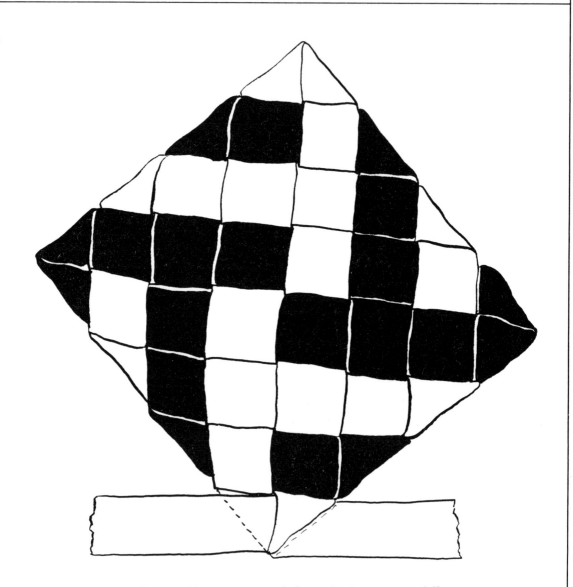

Repeat Step 6. You are now left with the two middle or
vertical bands. These will form the fourth and final corner. With the right-hand band on top, fold it *under* itself
on a 45° angle. Then, with the right-hand band overlapping the left, fold the right-hand band *over* the edge
of the mat to the other side and plait it down into the slot
made by the left band. Now, take the left-hand band and
fold it *over* to the top side of the mat, and plait it down
into the slot from which the right-hand band came.
Once you've cut and hidden the ends under a crosswise
element, the mat is finished.

Flat single-layer newspaper mats. 6" square (15.2 cm square). Two sampler newspaper mats, single-layer plaited, are shown against a plain-colored plaited mat from Italy. The design on the newspaper mats is achieved by plaiting a plain newspaper element as the first vertical band.

Contemporary plaited mat (petate). 46" x 68" (121.9 x 172.7 cm). Single-layer mat or "pe-tate" woven in Michoacán, Mexico. The mat is a two-over-two and one-over-three combination weave in flattened reeds.

The second sampler is two layers plaited simultaneously. You will need the same materials as were required to create the single-layer mat. This time, however, you will be using two sheets or both sides of a standard size newspaper. If the directions sound confusing, we have a word of advice. Try reading each step and accomplishing each turn as you proceed. Note that in forming corners, each band reverses itself twice so that it continues to plait in and out of the same layer on which it previously plaited.

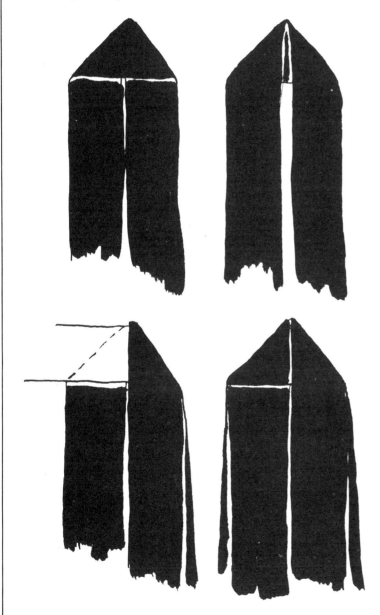

Take two sheets of newspaper and, as in the single-layer sampler, tear lengthwise strips at least 3″ to 4″ (7.6 to 10.2 cm) wide. You will need six bands, two of which should be colored black. Follow the directions for the single-layer plaited mat through Step 2. Take these two bands (black) and interlock them as shown above.

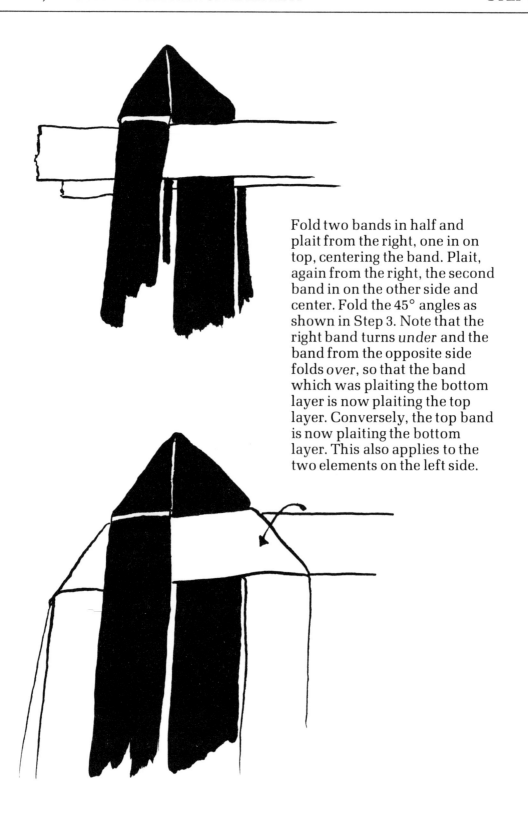

Fold two bands in half and plait from the right, one in on top, centering the band. Plait, again from the right, the second band in on the other side and center. Fold the 45° angles as shown in Step 3. Note that the right band turns *under* and the band from the opposite side folds *over*, so that the band which was plaiting the bottom layer is now plaiting the top layer. Conversely, the top band is now plaiting the bottom layer. This also applies to the two elements on the left side.

Plait in and center the next two bands, one on the top layer and the other on the bottom. Now, form two corners, one on either side. Fold the top right band *under* itself at a 45° angle. Fold the bottom right band *over* itself on a 45° angle. Next, fold this same band (bottom right) *under* itself 45° and, finally, fold the top right band *over* itself and the bottom right band on a 45° angle. On the left corner, fold the bottom band *over* itself on a 45° angle. Fold the top band *under* itself on a 45° angle, enclosing the bottom band. Fold the top band *over* itself at a 45° angle and fold the bottom band *under* itself, enclosing the top band.

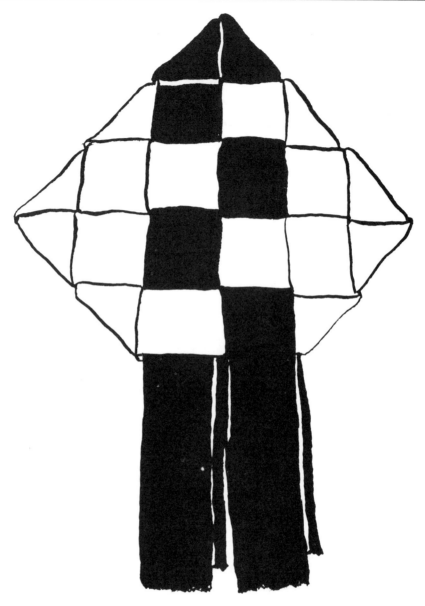

Now that you've created two new corners, plait the top left band over to meet the top right band and do the same on the bottom layer with those two bands. Taking the next two bands on the right, fold the top right band *under* itself on a 45° angle, and fold the bottom right band *over* itself on a 45° angle, enclosing the angle formed by the top band. On the left side, fold the bottom band *over* on a 45° angle. Fold the top left band *under* itself on a 45° angle and enclose the angle formed by the bottom band. Plait, on both the top and bottom layers, the left and right bands into each other so that they merge into one single element.

You are now left with four vertical bands; two on top and two on the bottom. Take the left bottom band, fold it *over* itself 45° and plait it in front of the top right band. Take the right bottom band and fold it *under* itself 45° and then *over* itself 45°, enclosing the left band. Tuck the right band down into the interior of the double surface. Fold the right top band *under* itself 45°, enclosing the right bottom band. Fold the top band *over* itself, again enclosing the bottom right band. Tuck the end into the same slot into which you tucked the lower right band.

Two vertical elements remain. Take the top left band, fold it 45° *under* itself, enclosing the two bands underneath. Fold this same band *over* itself 45°, enclosing the two underneath bands again. Plait the end down into the slot formed by tho top right band. Hide the end under the plaiting. The last element is folded 45° *under* itself, enclosing three bands, and is plaited down into the slot formed by the bottom right band. Again, tuck the end under the plaiting to neatly finish the piece.

Flat double-layer newspaper mat. 4¾″ square (12 cm square). The color pattern on this piece is achieved by plaiting the black elements in as the initial vertical strips.

Contemporary double-woven bag from the Philippines and contemporary double-woven change purse and money belt from Oaxaca, Mexico. Bag—15″ x 17½″ (38.1 x 44.5 cm), belt—2″ wide by 54″ long (5.1 x 137.2 cm), change purse—2¼″ x 2½″ (5.7 x 6.4 cm). (Left to right) A supple, double-plaited bag from the Philippines contains a money belt from Oaxaca, Mexico. The money belt is also double plaited and is worn under an outer belt of cloth. The change purse to the right is double plaited in red, green, and natural strands in order to achieve a patterned surface.

This sampler is intended to introduce you to the various shapes you might form by making corners at different intervals while working on a piece. It can be hung as a mobile for a child's room or used flat as a wallhanging or a placemat.

We used approximately 12 yards (11m) of cotton canvas webbing to create the shape. One band, 68″ (172.7 cm) long, was dyed red. Two bands, one 66″ (167.6 cm) long and the other 56″ (142.2 cm) long, were dyed navy blue. We used household dyes available at the drugstore. The webbing is heavily sized, so be sure to wash it thoroughly in soap and water before you attempt to dye it.

In the following illustrations, we have used black to show the red band and grey to show the blue bands.

To begin, take the red band and fold it in half lengthwise. Create the first corner by folding two 45° angles. Note that we have begun by folding the right side *under* itself and the left side *over* itself.

Plait in the 66″ (167.6 cm) navy-blue band, folding the right side 45° *under* itself, and the left side 45° *over* itself. Plait in a third band (white) approximately 20″ (50.8 cm) long. The fourth band, also white, must be about 18″ (45.7 cm) long, and will form two new corners. On the left side, turn the fourth band 45° *over* itself twice. On the right side, turn the band 45° *under* itself twice. Plait the two bands in until they merge. (We used straight pins to secure the ends of the bands together, and once the piece was completed, we tacked the ends with needle and threads, see Step 6.)

Turn the third band (white) *under* itself 45° on the right and *over* 45° on the left. Plait and merge these bands. Now, plait in the 56″ (142.2 cm) navy-blue band, turning the left corner 45° *over* itself and the right corner 45° *under* itself.

Plait in four white bands. The first one should be 27″ (68.6 cm) long, the second one 34″ (86.4 cm) long, the third one 34″ (86.4 cm) long, and the fourth one 28″ (71.1 cm) long.

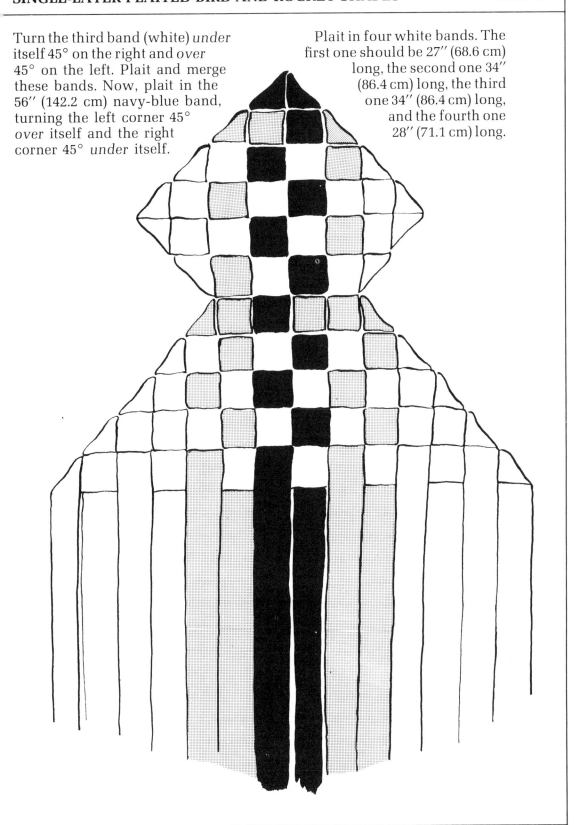

The fourth band makes two corners by turning the left side *over* itself twice at a 45° angle and the right side under itself twice. Plait these elements back in and allow them to merge, forming a new crosswise line of weaving.

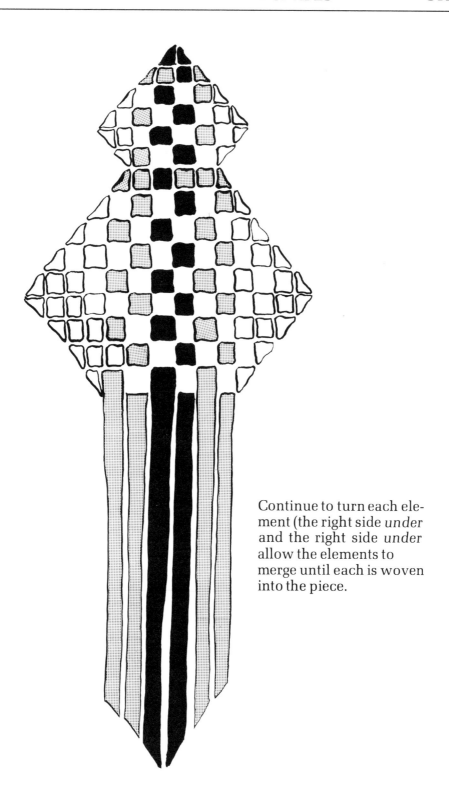

Continue to turn each element (the right side *under* and the right side *under* allow the elements to merge until each is woven into the piece.

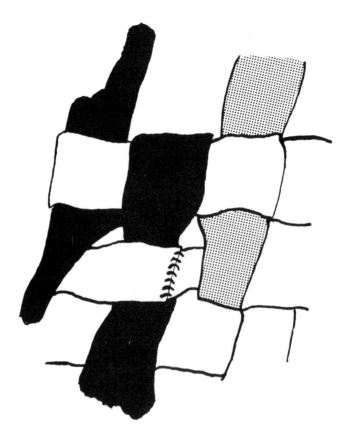

To tack the elements in place, allow the bands to overlap and then stay-stitch with needle and thread so neither the overlapping nor the attaching stitches are visible. If you wish to use the sampler as a wallhanging or a placemat, this would be the finishing touch.

To shape the piece in order to
achieve the rocket shape shown in
the photograph, simply tack the two
largest corners together. We attached fishline to the corner and
hung the piece as a mobile.

(Left) Single-layer plaited Bird or Rocket shape. 30" longest length and 14½" at widest point (76.2 x 36.8 cm). This piece is created of cotton canvas webbing. Some elements were dyed red, others blue, so the piece expresses a patriotic theme in color. It can be laid flat on a table with the ends allowed to hang over the edge, creating a unique placemat.

(Above) Single-layer plaited Bird or Rocket shape. 30" longest length and 14½" at widest point (76.2 x 36.8 cm). This is the same piece as shown in the preceding photograph, however, Step 7 was followed and the piece became three-dimensional.

We used two skins of goatskin suede to plait this pillow. Each skin (one beige and one brown) measured approximately 5 square feet (.4 square meters) and had been tanned with a process which renders the leather handwashable. The skins are 2 ounce (56.7 gram) garment suede. We found that the total yardage necessary to complete the project was 12 yards (11m) half brown, half beige.

In order to obtain the design shown in the photograph, we plaited in opposite colors. In other words, a brown band was plaited in on the top layer, and a beige band was plaited in on the bottom layer. We then alternated—beige on top, brown on the bottom—and continued to alternate throughout the plaiting process.

Masking tape secured the edges as we plaited and we stuffed the piece with washable polyester fiber. We also used leather glue to add on to those bands which needed to have additional length as well as to finish off the bands as they merged in the weaving procedure. (Leather glue bonds except when dry cleaned. If you intend to dry clean your pillow, we suggest that you use a glover's needle and nylon thread to staystitch the bands.) As you plait, you will sense the logic in forming the sides. The band which plaits on the bottom turns over itself and begins to plait on the top and vice versa.

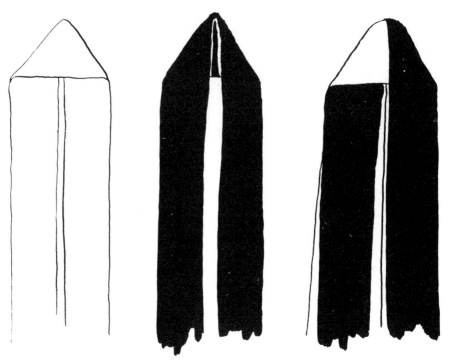

Cut the skins into 1" (2.5 cm) wide bands. (You will need 15 bands of brown and 15 bands of beige.) Fold and interlock one beige and one brown band as shown. Each of the two bands should measure at least 20" (50.8 cm) when folded in half.

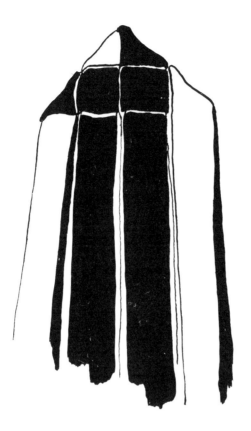

With the vertical bands forming
the first corner, plait in a brown
band on top and a beige band on
the bottom. On the left side, fold
the beige band *over* itself on a 45°
angle and fold the brown band
under itself, enclosing the beige
band. On the right side, fold the
brown band *under* itself, enclosing the brown band. Use the
masking tape to secure the bands
as you plait in the next two strips
of leather.

This time, plait the beige on top and the brown on the bottom layer. On the left side, fold the brown band *over* itself on a 45° angle and fold the beige band *under* itself, enclosing the brown band. On the right side, fold the beige band *under* itself 45° and the brown band *over* itself, enclosing the beige band. The third band of plaiting is brown on top and beige on the bottom. On the left side, fold the beige band *over* itself 45° and the brown band *under* itself, enclosing the beige strip. The right side is formed by turning the brown band *under* itself 45° and the beige band *over* itself, enclosing the brown band.

Continue plaiting in four more bands on the top and bottom layers, alternating the colors as we have indicated. After plaiting in the additional bands, you will have plaited a total of seven bands down from the top corner. On the left, you have turned the beige band *over* itself 45° and the brown band *under* itself, enclosing the beige. On the right, you have folded the brown band *under* itself and the beige band *over* itself, enclosing the brown.

To form the corner, take the brown band and fold it *over* itself 45°
and fold the beige band *under* itself, enclosing the brown band. On
the right, you have formed the side by folding the brown band *under*
itself 45° and the beige band *over* itself, enclosing the brown band.
To form this corner, fold the beige band *under* itself 45° and fold the
brown band *over* itself, enclosing the beige band. The brown bands
now plait across to merge and form the eighth band of weaving on
the top layer. The two beige bands perform the same function on the
bottom layer.

Plait in four more bands on both the top and bottom layers. Secure all edges with masking tape and, at this point, stuff the pillow with the polyester fibers. (It is best to overstuff the piece slightly so that there will be adequate filling for the extra two bands and corner necessary to complete the form.)

Plait in the last two bands on the top and bottom layers. At this point, you have four vertical bands left: two brown on top and two beige on the bottom. Take the left bottom band, fold it *over* itself 45°, and plait it in front of the top right band. Take the right bottom band and fold it *under* itself 45° and then *over* itself 45°, enclosing the left band. Tuck the right band down into the interior of the double surface. Fold the right top band *under* itself 45°, enclosing the right bottom band. Fold this same top band *over* itself again, enclosing the bottom right band. Tuck the end into the same slot in which you tucked the lower right band.

You are now left with two elements, both on the top layer. Take the top left band and fold it 45° *under* itself, enclosing the two bands underneath. Fold this same band *over* itself 45°, enclosing the two underneath bands again. Plait the end down into the slot formed by the top right band. Hide the end under the plaiting and glue to the under element. The last element is folded 45° *under* itself, enclosing three bands, and is plaited down into the slot formed by the bottom right band. Again, conceal the end under the plaiting. Glue it to the underneath element and you are finished!

(Above) Double-layer plaited pillow. 11½"
square (29.2 cm square). This photograph
shows the bottom layer or underside of the
double-layer plaited pillow. Note the alternate pattern formed by the light and
dark elements.

(Right) Soft cubes by Susan Jamart. 4"
square (10.2 cm square). Strong black-
and-white verticals, horizontals, and
diagonals crisscross the surface of these
cubes.

Double-layer plaited basket from Patzcuaro, Mexico. 9″ square at base, 9″ high (22.9 cm square x 22.9 cm). This sturdy, double-layer plaited basket is woven in a combination one-over-two, one-over-three, and one-over-one weave. This type of basket is, like the mats, a staple item in many Mexican homes.

4

SHAPING PLAITED FORMS

Achieving a three-dimensional form in the plaiting technique is basically quite simple. We've found single- and double-layer plaited baskets in all shapes and sizes, some soft and pliant, some stiff and coarse.

The single-layer silverplate basket from Mexico exhibits the use of a plaint, yet sturdy material. It is plaited in a two-over-two weave up to 1½″ (3.8 cm) from the top. There, the artisan plaited one element over five elements and secured the bands by returning to a two-over-two weave as the elements were woven back down into the interior of the basket. The lidded shopping bag plaited in Hawaii is also single-layer plaited in pandanus fibers. It is a sturdy yet supple material with which to plait.

Double-layer plaiting in the shaped form has usually been employed to add strength to a piece. The basket from Patzcuaro, Mexico, plaited in flattened bamboo strips, aptly illustrates this point.

The trick to creating form lies in mastering the creation of corners. Once you've done this, you will be able to create symmetrical or unsymmetrical shapes. The computer-tape forms shown in the Ideas and Design chapter are excellent examples of the possibilities inherent in the plaited form.

The size and width of the shapes you make are determined by the size of the elements you wish to use in the weaving. The number of elements, either horizontal or vertical, also contributes to the size of the final form.

In this chapter, we will show you how to plait a simple basket of newspaper strips—perfect for recycled Easter baskets—a closed rectangular cube form, a double-layer plaited basket of grosgrain ribbon, and finally, a basket and lid of braided coconut fibers.

Let's begin!

The first three-dimensional sampler incorporates the plaiting of corners at the base. Note the color pattern which is formed as the light and dark elements shape the basket form.

To create this sampler you will need three sheets of standard-size newspaper, straight pins, a magic marker or felt-tip pen and, if you wish, a pair of scissors.

Take three sheets of newspaper and, as in the previous flat samplers, tear or cut lengthwise strips 3″ to 4″ (7.6 to 10.2 cm) wide. You will need eight bands, four of which should be colored black. Take one black band and one plain newspaper band and fold each in half lengthwise. Lay the bands across one another as shown. (The fold lines mark the midpoint, both horizontally and vertically.)

Plait in (one-under, one-over) the remaining six bands. To center the strips perfectly, place two black bands horizontally above the initial black band and one black band below. Vertically plait one newsprint band to the right of the initial strip and two newsprint bands to the left. Place straight pins in each of the four corners to secure the weave.

Take the top four vertical
bands and, with the right-of-
center band, begin plaiting
(one-over, one-under), as
shown. Secure the top point
with a straight pin.

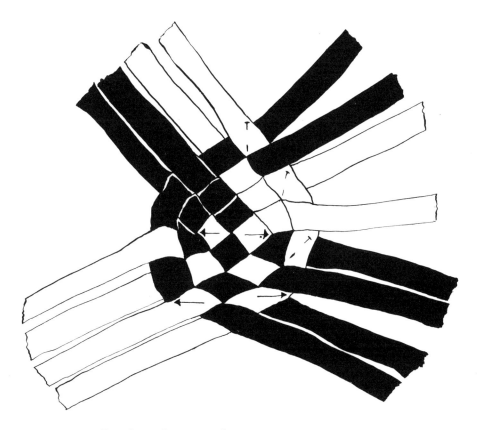

Continue forming the corners, moving around the piece from right to left. As you plait you will see that each of the corners is formed in the center of the four flat-plaited bands. As each corner is formed, the elements automatically plait up the sides of the shape in a diagonal form. The arrows in the illustration above indicate the two corners already formed as well as the two corners yet to be plaited.

Continue plaiting until there
are at least three diamonds
formed above each of the
four corners.

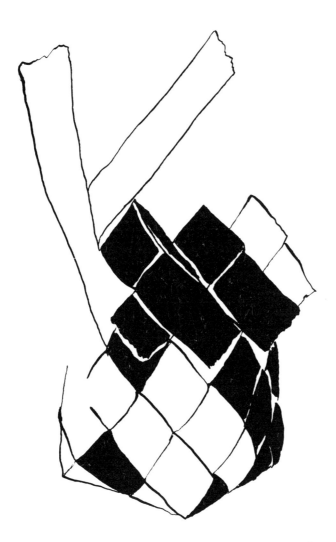

To finish the basket in a saw-tooth-edge pattern, fold one left element back over the next element on the right side. Fold the right element over the left and plait each band down into the appropriate slot to secure the edges. Once all the edges are secure, re-move all the straight pins. In the plain newspaper basket, we hid all the ends under the plaiting. In the sampler, we added a decorative touch by allowing the ends to remain outside the weaving. We also slit the exposed ends to form a fringe.

Single-layer newspaper basket. 3″ square at base, 5″ high at top of sawtooth edge (7.6 x 12.7 cm). This sampler exhibits the design possibilities inherent in using two varied elements in plaiting. The edge at the top has been finished off in a herringbone or sawtooth and the bands are fringed.

Plaited silverplate basket from Mexico. 4″ square at base, 4″ high (11.4 x 7.3 cm).
Plaited shopping bag from Hawaii. 11½″ x 6″ at base, 8½″ high (29.2 x 15.2 x 21.6 cm).
Both the shopping bag from Hawaii and the silverplate basket from Mexico exhibit the
use of pliant, yet sturdy plaiting elements. Each piece is single-layer plaited.

We used braided coconut fiber from Hawaii to create this piece. It is sold in skeins and one skein is more than sufficient to plait both the basket and the lid. The material is coarse in texture but is very pliant. We used straight pins to secure the elements and tweezers to pull the bands back into the piece as we turned the edges at the top.

Each strip was precut to measure 30″ (76.2 cm) in length. We used 56 lengths—24 for the basket and 32 for the lid. The braided fiber has a dimension of approximately ¼″ (.6 cm); therefore, we added the extra lengths in the lid so that it would fit well over the top of the basket. If you choose to use a different material to create this piece, take into account the dimension of the elements when planning the number of bands necessary to create the lid.

To make this piece as we have done, you will need one skein of braided coconut fiber (see Supplier's List), straight pins, scissors, and tweezers.

Cut 56 lengths of fiber, each 30″ (76.2 cm) long. Take 24 elements and plait 12 on the horizontal and 12 on the vertical, following Steps 1 through 6 of the Single-Layer Plaited Basket. (We plaited up 15 diamonds at each corner to give the basket height.)

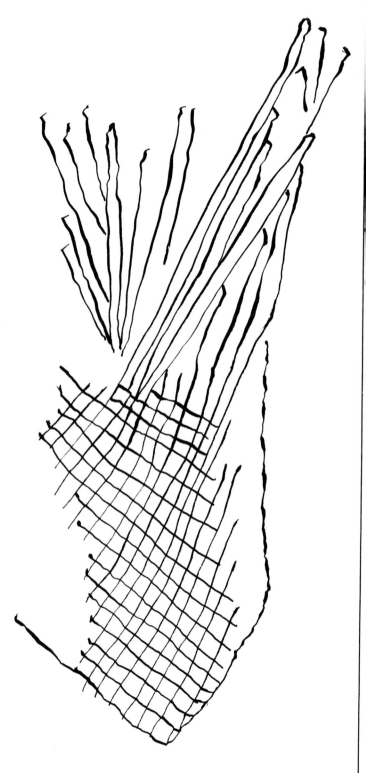

Using the tweezers, pull the bands
down through the slots on the exterior of the basket. (We plaited these
ends down five blocks.) Cut the ends
evenly and unply and unspin the
fibers to create a fringe.

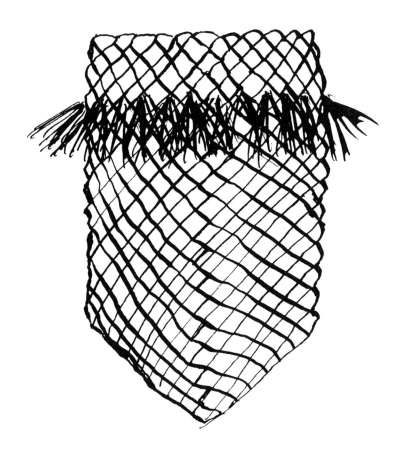

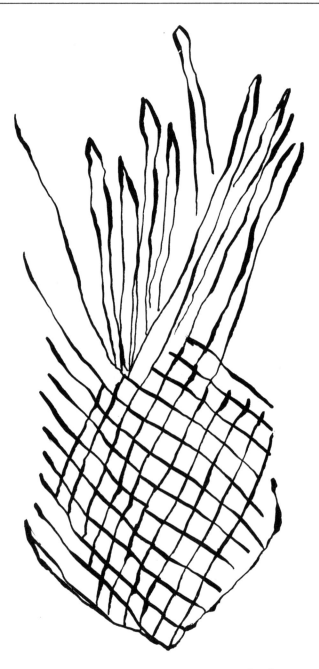

Plait the remaining 32 elements, which will form the lid. Use 16 bands on the horizontal and 16 on the vertical. Again follow Steps 1 through 6 of the Single-Layer Plaited Basket. (This time we plaited up nine diamonds at each corner.)

Again, using the tweezers, pull the bands down through 12 slots on the exterior of the basket. (We used five blocks previously, but this time we want to create the fringe at the bottom of the form.) Cut the ends evenly and unply; then unspin the fibers to form the fringe.

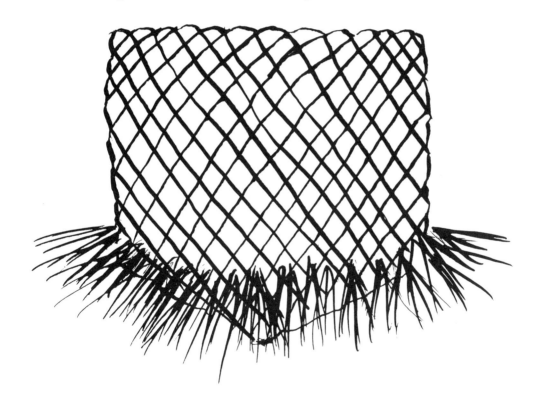

(Above) Basket and lid of braided coconut fiber. 3″ square at base, 8″ high (7.6 cm square x 20.3 cm). The lid measures 4″ square (10.2 cm square) at the top and is large enough to fit down over the edge of the basket.

(Right) Lidded basket of braided coconut fibers. 3″ square at the base, 8″ high (7.6 cm square x 20.3 cm). This basket and lid were plaited of braided coconut fiber. The bands were fringed at the edges.

This second sampler dealing with the creation of form is a rectangular cube. In this series of steps, we will show you how to create a closed shape. We chose to do a rectangular cube form, but you could achieve a perfect cube by simply plaiting up only two diamonds from each corner as opposed to plaiting three as we did. The materials necessary to complete this sampler are three standard-size sheets of newspaper, straight pins, a magic marker or felt-tip pen, and, if you wish, scissors.

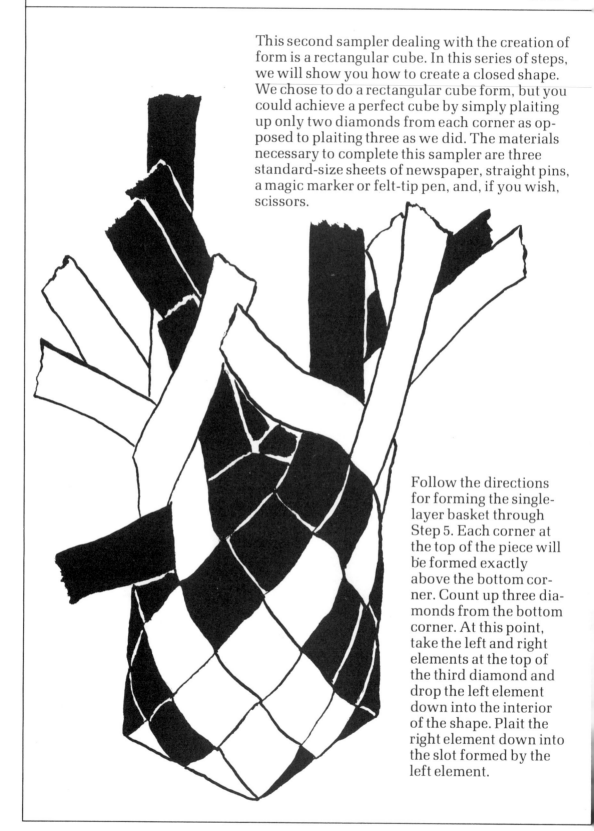

Follow the directions for forming the single-layer basket through Step 5. Each corner at the top of the piece will be formed exactly above the bottom corner. Count up three diamonds from the bottom corner. At this point, take the left and right elements at the top of the third diamond and drop the left element down into the interior of the shape. Plait the right element down into the slot formed by the left element.

Continue around the top of the shape,
forming three more corners exactly
above the bottom corners. Tuck each of
the ends which are plaiting on the exterior under the weave so that the ends are
hidden. Having used two of the elements
to plait each of the four corners, you are
now left with eight elements.

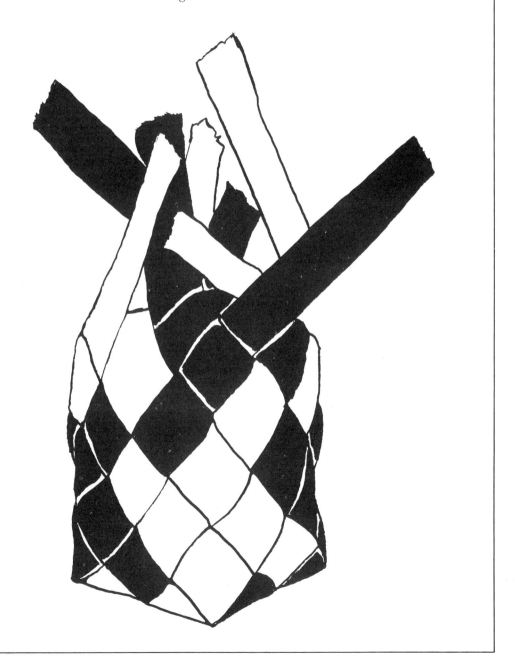

Take the left element nearest you and plait it across the top of the shape to merge with the element weaving across from the right.

Plait in and merge the remaining six elements until a flat surface is obtained. Cut off any remaining ends and the rectangular cube is complete.

Single-layer plaited rectangular cube form. 3″ square at the base, 4¼″ high (7.6 cm square x 10.8 cm). Note the color pattern formed at the top of the shape. This is achieved by plaiting all the black strips on the horizontal and all the plain newspaper strips on the vertical when you begin.

We've used the double-layer technique in this sampler for two purposes: first, to add body to the ribbon elements, and second, to make use of the color, texture, and design possibilities inherent in using two materials simultaneously.

The piece has been woven in one throughout. In other words, the plain and patterned elements have been treated as though they were a single strip. We deviate from this double element only at the top of the form where it is necessary to separate the elements in order to achieve the finished edge.

To create this shape you will need 24 yards (22m) of grosgrain ribbon; half of the plain and half of the patterned. Each of the 24 strips were precut to measure exactly 1 yard (.9m). We used straight pins to secure the ends as we plaited.

Cut the plain and patterned ribbon into 24 lengths, each 1 yard (.9m) long. Take one plain band and one patterned band and fold together lengthwise to obtain the midpoint. Take a second group (one plain and one patterned) and again fold lengthwise to obtain the midpoint. Proceed to plait one group as the horizontal band and the second group as the vertical band. Secure the two bands at the center with a straight pin.

As shown above, each set of two elements plaits together as one. (We've used white to show the plain band and black to show the patterned band.)

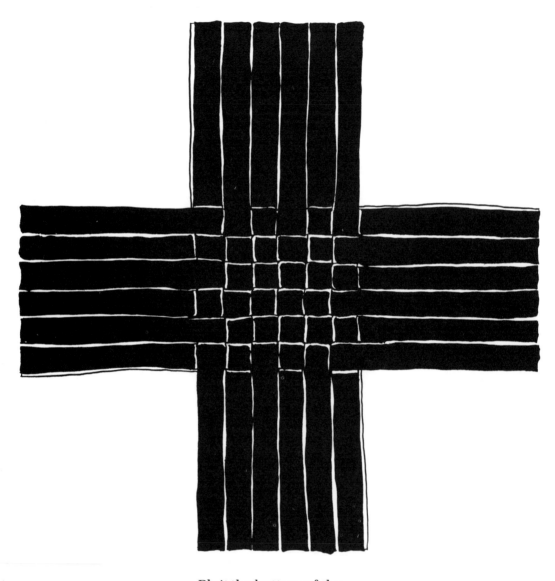

Plait the bottom of the
basket as shown. You will
have six elements on the
horizontal and six on the
vertical.

Create the corners as shown in Steps 3 and 4 of the
Single-Layer Plaited Basket. (Each corner will be
made at the midpoint of the six vertical or six horizontal elements.) Continue plaiting up the sides until
you have three full diamonds above each corner as
shown above.

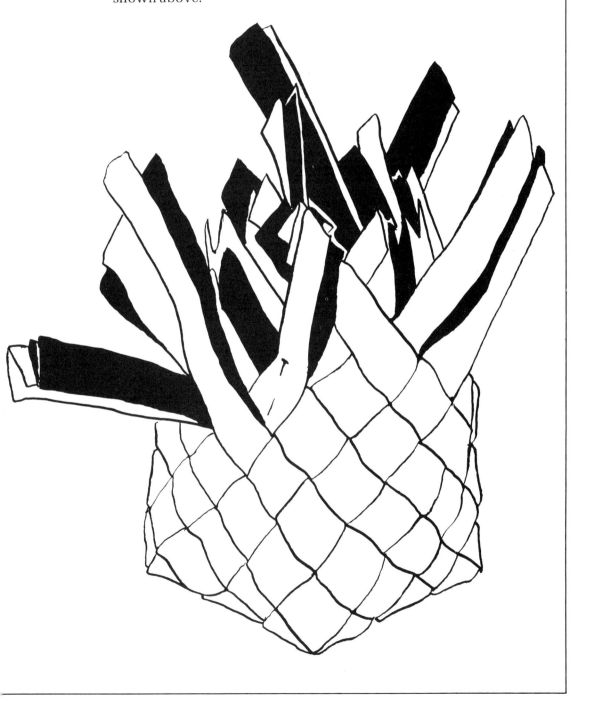

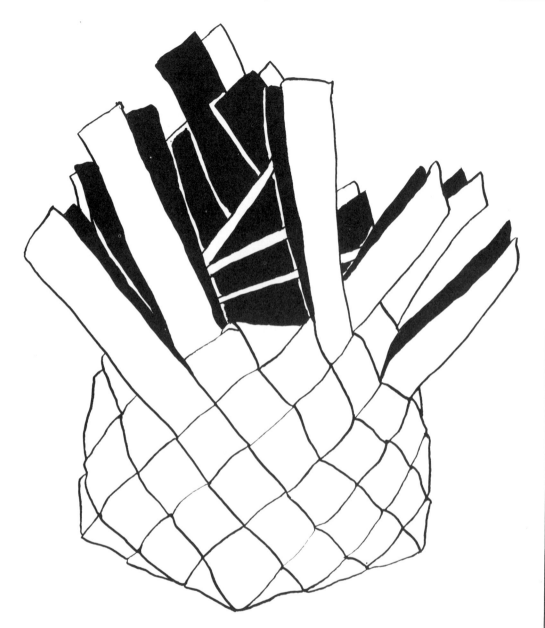

Select a corner to begin creating the edge. At the top of the third diamond, fold the left element *under* itself at a 45° angle and allow the band to drop down into the interior of the basket. Take the right element and fold it *under* itself at a 45° angle, enclosing the left element. Note that, unlike the previous basket sampler, you are creating a flat edge as opposed to a sawtooth or herringbone edge. Secure the bands with straight pins as you turn the edge.

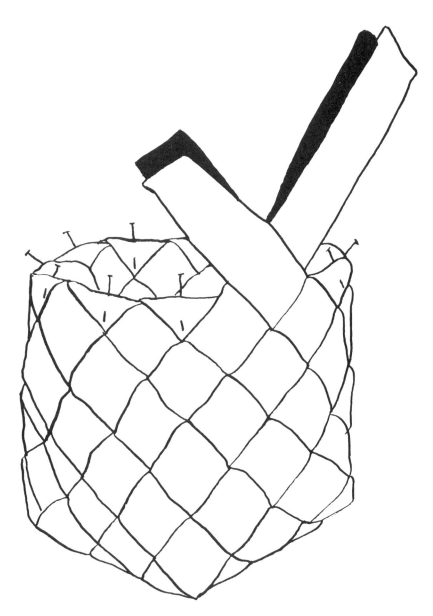

Continue creating the edge, folding first the left element 45° *under* itself and the right element 45° *under* itself, enclosing the left. As you make the edge, continue to secure the bands with straight pins. Once you've completed the edge, plait the plain bands over and under each other, covering the patterned bands.

To finish off the interior, we chose to turn each left
and right plain band back under the other two and
one-half blocks down from the edge, as shown above.
We then stay-stitched the bands to the patterned elements directly under them.

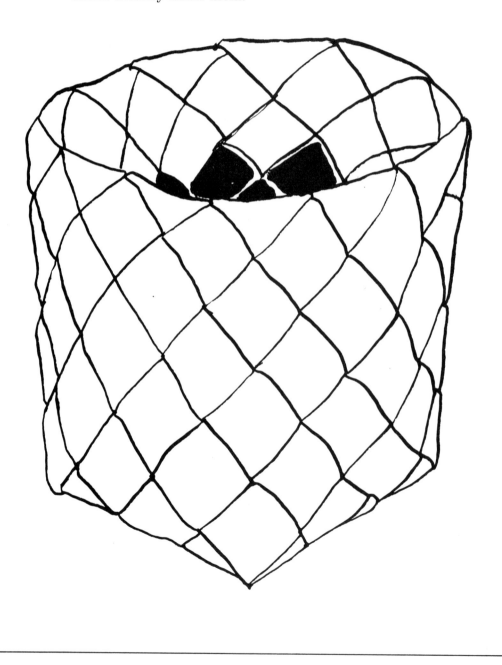

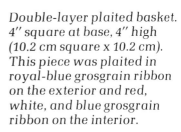

Double-layer plaited basket.
4" square at base, 4" high
(10.2 cm square x 10.2 cm).
This piece was plaited in
royal-blue grosgrain ribbon
on the exterior and red,
white, and blue grosgrain
ribbon on the interior.

Interior view of double-
plaited ribbon basket. Note
the pattern within a pattern
formed by the tricolored ele-
ments.

Contemporary lidded basket from mainland China. 11″ diameter, 6″ high (27.9 x 15.2 cm). This particular lidded basket features hexagonal plaiting on the top layer of the lid. The underside is plaited in the one-over-two and one-over-three pattern shown on the interior of the basket. Photo by Jon Westfall.

HEXAGONAL PLAITING

Hexagonal or three-element plaiting is by far the most exciting of all the plaited forms in terms of color, texture, and design possibilities. It is also the most difficult to achieve. However, if you follow step-by-step the directions for creating the next basket form, you will be able to understand the movement of the elements in both flat hexagonal plaiting (the bottom of the shape), and cylindrical hexagonal plaiting (the sides of the form).

Single-layer three-element basket. 12″ diameter, 7″ deep (30.5 x 17.8 cm). This sampler was hexagonally plaited in 1½″ wide (3.8 cm) black and gray belting and transparent plastic strips. It is a pliant, yet sturdy container.

We chose to use 1½″ (3.8 cm) rug binding, which comes in 36 yard (32.8 m) rolls. You will need 10 yards (9.1 m) of the gray and 10 yards (9.1 m) of the black. We bought the plastic in sheet form and cut each of the eight elements 1½″ (3.8 cm) wide. The plastic is approximately the same weight as the rug binding, insuring a uniformity in the structure of the finished piece.

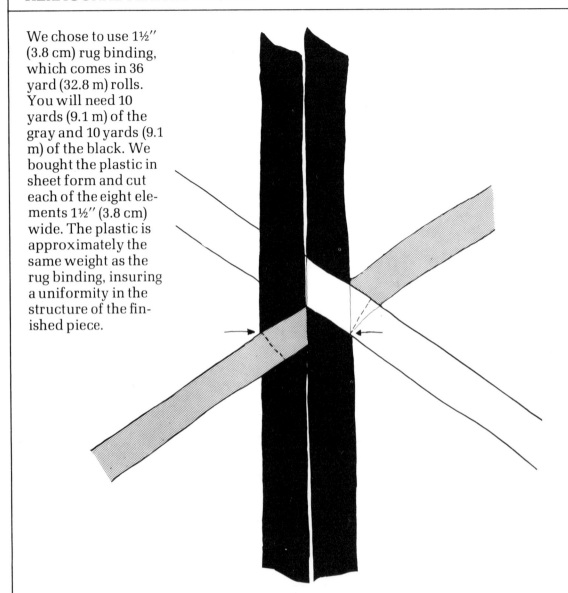

Cut the black and gray rug binding into eight lengths, each 40″ (101.6 cm) long. Cut the plastic sheet into eight strips, each 1½″ (3.8 cm) wide and 40″ (101.6 cm) long. Fold two black elements in half lengthwise to mark the midpoints. (The arrows in the illustration above indicate the midpoint on each of the vertical elements.) *Over* the right black band lay the transparent element at a 30° angle, matching midpoint to mid-

point at the far right side of the black elements. This transparent band plaits *under* the left black vertical band as shown. From the left, plait the first gray band in *over* the left black band and *under* both the black band on the right and the transparent band. The angle formed by these four bands will be repeated in the diamond shapes indigenous to the flat hexagonal plait.

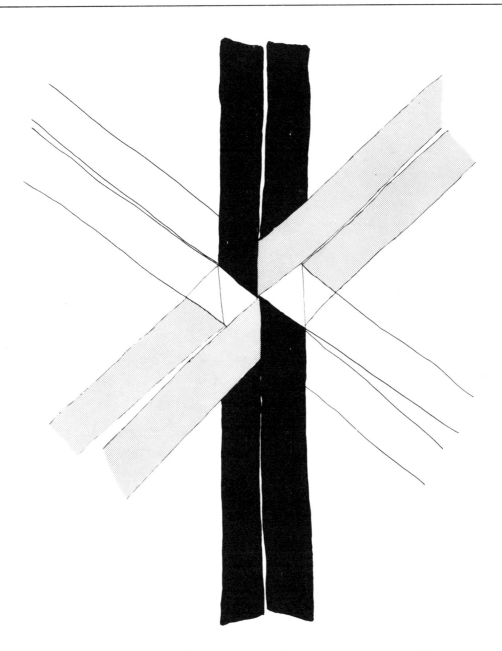

From the top right, plait in a second gray band *over* the right black band and the transparent band, and *under* the left black band. From the bottom right, plait in a second transparent band *under* the black and gray elements to the right and *over* the black and gray to the left. Note that this band also plaits *under* one gray element on the left.

Working in a counterclockwise direction, add a third vertical black band to the right side of your plaiting. Working from bottom to top, plait this band *under* the two transparent bands and *over* the two gray bands. Enter a transparent band next from the right middle and, working from right to left, plait *under* the two gray bands and black band, and *over* the two black bands on the left.

We break with our *over*-two, *under*-two pattern here because
we are dealing with three vertical black bands and three diagonal transparent bands. Take a third gray band and from the
upper right, plait *over* one black, *under* two black and *under*
one transparent, and *over* two transparent bands. From the top
left, enter the fourth vertical black band and plait it *over* one
transparent band, *under* one gray and two transparent bands,
and *over* two gray bands.

The fourth transparent band now plaits in from the middle left. Plait it *over* one gray, *under* two gray and one black, and then *over* three black bands. Enter the fourth gray band from the lower left, and plait it *over* one black band, *under* two black bands and one transparent band, and finally, *over* one black band two transparent bands and *under* the last transparent band. Take the far right vertical black element and, from the bottom, lift it out and over the transparent band covering it.

Enter the fifth black band from the lower right of the piece. Plait it *over* the first transparent band, *under* the second transparent band, *over* the third transparent and first gray bands, *under* the fourth transparent and second gray bands, *over* the third gray band and *over* the fourth gray band.

Enter the fifth transparent band at the middle right of the piece.
Plait it *over* a gray band, *under* one gray and *over* one black,
over one black and one gray, *over* the next black and gray
bands, *under* one gray and *over* one black, *under* one black and
one gray, *over* one black and *under* the last black band. Take
the farthest black element to the right and at the top, lift it out
and *over* the top the gray band.

Plait in the fifth gray band from the top right. The band moves *under* three black elements, *over* one black and two transparent bands, *under* one black and *over* one transparent, *under* one black and *under* one transparent, *over* and *under* the next two transparent bands. Lift the top left transparent band out and *over* the black element to the top left of the piece.

Enter the sixth black vertical from the top left. Plait it *under* three transparent bands, *over* one gray and one transparent, *over* one gray and *under* one transparent, *under*, *over*, and *under* the last three gray bands. Lift the top gray band on the middle left out and plait it *over* the last transparent band.

Enter the sixth transparent band from the middle left and plait *under* three gray bands, *over* one gray and one black, *over* the next black and *under* one gray, *under* one black and one gray, *over* one black, and *under* two blacks. Take the lower left black element and lift it out and plait it *over* the last gray band.

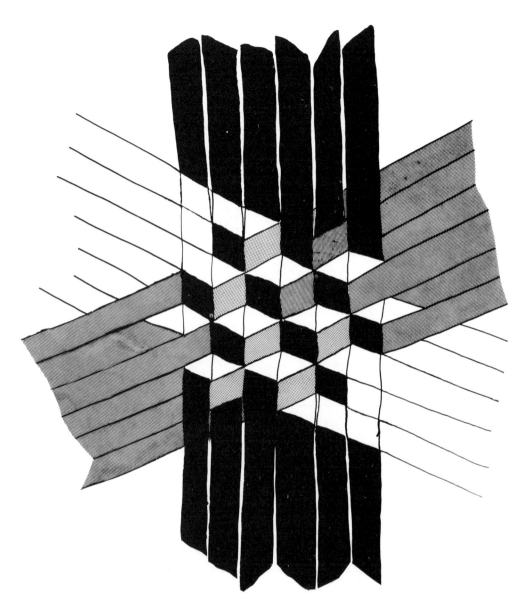

Take the first gray band on the middle right and lift it out and
over the first transparent band adjacent to it. Plait in the sixth
gray band from the bottom left. Weave this element in *under*
three black, *over* two transparent and one black, *over* one
transparent and *under* one black, *under* one black and one
transparent, and *over* three transparent elements. Take the two
transparent elements to the bottom right and lift them out and
over the black elements. The bottom band moves out *over* two
elements and the second transparent band moves out *over* one
black element.

Plait in the seventh black vertical element from the bottom right of the piece. This band moves *under* one transparent, *over* two transparent bands, *under* one gray and one transparent, *under* the next transparent and *over* the gray, *over* one gray and one transparent and *under* three gray bands. Take the top transparent band on the middle right and plait it out *over* the last gray band on the middle right.

Plait in the seventh transparent band from the top middle right. Move the element in *under* two gray bands, *over* one gray and one black, *under* one gray and *over* one black, *under* a second gray and black, *under* one gray and *over* one black, *over* one black and one gray, and *under* three black bands. Lift the top right gray band out and *over* the last two black verticals on the top right.

Enter the seventh gray band from the top right. Plait *under* three black bands, *over* one transparent and one black, *under* the second transparent and *under* the black, *under* the second transparent and the next black band, *over* the third transparent and the last black band, *over* the fourth transparent, and *under* the final three transparent bands. Take the top left black vertical band and lift it out and *over* the last two transparent bands.

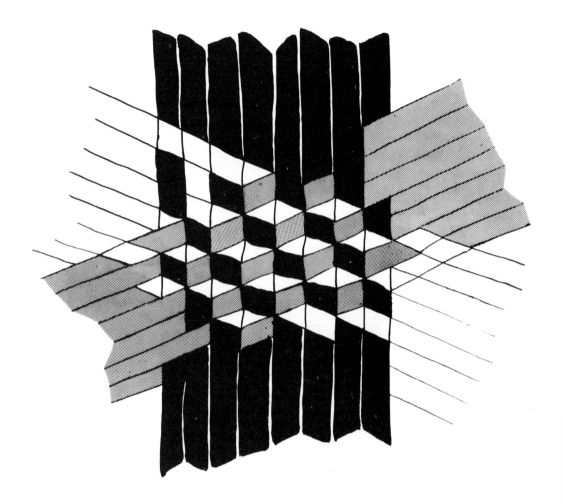

Plait in the eighth vertical black band from the top left. Plait *over* two transparent bands, *under* one transparent, *over* one transparent and one gray, *over* one gray and *under* one transparent, *under* one gray and one transparent, *over* one gray and one transparent, *over* one transparent and one gray, and *under* the next three gray bands. Take the bottom transparent band on the left side and lift it out and plait it *over* the last two gray bands.

Enter the eighth transparent band from the lower left middle of
the piece. Plait *under* three gray bands, *over* one gray and one
black, *over* one black and *under* one gray, *under* one black and
one gray, *under* one gray and *over* one black, *over* one black
and one gray, and *under* the next four black elements. Lift the
last gray band at the bottom left out and *over* the two black verticals on the left. Take the top right transparent band and lift it
out and *over* the last gray band at middle right.

Plait in the eighth gray band from the bottom left. This element weaves *over* one black, *under* two black bands, *over* one black and one transparent, *under* one transparent and *under* one black, *under* one black and one transparent, *over* one transparent and one black, *over* one transparent and *under* one black, *under* one transparent and one black, and *over* the last three transparent bands. Take the last two verticals on the bottom right and lift them out and *over* the last two transparent bands. The third transparent band lifts out and *over* the far right black vertical. The six arrows on the illustration above indicate the placement of the corners.

We created the first corner at the lower left and worked clock-wise. To begin, think in terms of creating a five-pointed star with three of the points on the top and two of the points on the side of the piece. In this case, reading from left to right, the three points on the top will be black, gray, and then trans-parent. The two points on the side will be gray and then black, again reading from left to right. Take the second vertical black band and plait it 45° to the right *under* the first and second gray bands and *under* the third black band. Take the first black ver-tical to the left and plait it *under* the first gray band and second black band. The arrow indicates the heart or axis of the five-pointed star.

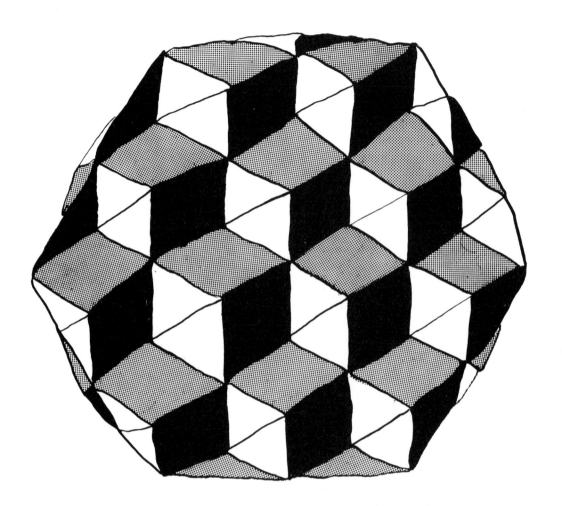

Continue creating the corners in numerical order, working in a
clockwise direction. Take the band to the left of the axis point
and plait it 45° to the right *under* the two adjacent bands. Once
you've plaited all the corners, you're ready to weave up the
sides.

Turn the piece so that the unplaited ends are on top. Holding a corner towards you, grasp the two vertical bands and plait the first diagonal on the left *under* these two verticals and *over* the third vertical to the right. The diagonal band coming from the right plaits *under* the right vertical and *over* the next two verticals. Plait up two diagonal bands on each corner.

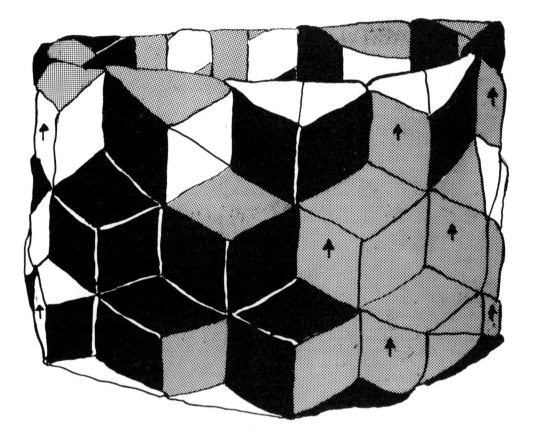

The sides of the piece now begin to take shape as one continuous series of hexagonal cubes comprised of three elements. Each vertical band is crossed by a diagonal from the right, then the left, then the right, before the vertical is again exposed. (The arrows on the illustration indicate the gray and transparent vertical elements.) To finish the edge, we measured up 8″ (20.3 cm) from each corner and folded the ends into the interior. Using the black banding, we machine-stitched the edge as shown in the photograph above.

Three-weft plaited basket by Susan Jamart, 1973. 8″ diameter, 6″ high (20.3 x 15.2 cm). This piece functions as soft sculpture. The artist has plaited the ends back into the side of the form and the interior is slightly stuffed to retain its shape. The elements are ⅝″ (1.6 cm) strips of grosgrain ribbon. Collection of Carol Westfall.

Plaited vest by Judy Krall. Gold wallpaper was used to plait this vest. A unique use of material. The piece is pliant and very comfortable to wear.

IDEAS AND DESIGN

We envision many ways in which plaiting can be utilized as a fiber-art form, especially without the historical limitations imposed by function. The traditional examples seem to be limited by utilitarian form and restricted by the available natural materials. Both restrictions can give a positive guide within which to work, but can also preclude investigation of the many other possibilities. In every country, mats or containers make up the bulk of traditional plaiting. Without this design restriction, the subtle variations in old pieces can be used and changed in scale to become stronger, flexible, and more personal. The design range is thereby enormous.

In order to expand the limits of the plaited form, it is helpful not to think of plaiting in distinct categories. Forget the dividing line between flat or shaped pieces, empty or stuffed, parallel- or diagonal-plaited. Once you have mastered the techniques, you will see how they can move from one to the other as you search for a certain line or surface.

BODY

Of the many factors which influence a plaited piece, obviously the material is important, not just for ease of handling, correct length, and color, but for body. A piece plaited with cloth strips will be radically different from the same design made out of stiff oak-tag paper. When designing large three-dimensional constructions, keep in mind that a stiff material will maintain a greater height and volume. Alternating stiff and soft materials within a piece can give interesting gentle pockets contrasted with hard areas.

JOINS

If the piece is on a large scale, short elements must have additions. Natural vegetable materials usually have one rough side which helps to hold an added strip in place as it is overlapped onto the strand before it. This advantage is often lacking in contemporary materials. Some of the best plaiting strips, like ribbon, are very slippery. We suggest several new solutions. The most dramatic is to tie an obvious knot and incorporate it into the piece. On a very textured, lumpy surface this works well, but on a smooth, sleek piece discreet tacking with needle and thread is often preferable. The stitching can always be hidden under an overlapping strand of plaiting. A third alternative is to incorporate temporary fastenings such as straight pins, safety pins or paperclips into the piece and leave them as a structural part of the design.

SOURCES OF INSPIRATION

When a piece is in progress, it can be changed and reworked. Cut it, stretch it, turn it inside out, and then continue working with this new form. The technique is only interesting as long as it functions and moves in the way you want it to. Try pushing the technique until you can make it follow your ideas and directions.

Setting forth a problem to be solved is an excellent source of inspiration. We find this method to be most challenging. Define the limits of this self-imposed assignment until it seems almost impossible. Then begin. The problem can center on a limitation of material, finished surface, or method of presentation. For example, construct a plaited piece which will move from the floor up the wall or vice versa, but with both floor and wall sections equally important visually. Limit the materials to one kind and two colors; add a third nonstructural element such as string that will be free to move in and out of the plaiting. Define the edges as straight or irregular and start!

Another possible departure point is to construct a fragment. Many ancient textile specimens are pieces of larger unknown items which have deteriorated, frequently leaving the mystery of an incomplete design or a partial shape. What is implied can make a stronger visual image than the actual piece. Look at fragments of art objects—sculpture, textiles, etc.—in museums and books until you feel their mystery. Then work on a piece that will never be finished but will stop at a point where the shape and design are complete as a fragment but imply something more.

Ideas flow most freely when you are comfortable with the technical aspects of plaiting, so practice on samples is important. As you plait, the structure of the technique will itself suggest ways to move. You will begin to see the pattern formed by the plaiting itself and can follow this away from the original basket structure. You can then begin moving beyond the known shapes into areas where the forms of plaiting are open to exploration.

We have made lists of design possibilities for different aspects of plaiting.

As you work in the technique, these can be used as jumping-off points for continued private investigation.

FLAT PLAITING

Flat plaiting can define spaces from geometric areas to anthropomorphic forms; it is not limited to rectangular mat shapes. Flat-plaited pieces make excellent construction elements for larger pieces.

To be really free to use flat plaiting in its most complete definition, you may consider it as a raw material for a form. It can be cut, bunched, and tied until it moves in the desired direction.

Harry Boom, a European artist, plaits clear plastic strips in squares which, from a distance, appear flat; however, on closer examination, there are subtle irregularities in the surface like small hills, sometimes only one in a piece. These transform the surface very subtly by casting a small shadow and changing the quality of the light reflection on the shiny elements.

The following list suggests starting points for flat plaiting:

1. Plait a flat piece and work the ends back toward the center. Then pass string through the edge and pull it into a new shape.

2. Make one of several flat pieces into another shape by folding, pinching, gathering, etc.

3. Turn corners in unusual places to vary the outside edge. (Two-dimensional animal forms are plaited this way in Mexico and Egypt.)

4. Plait many long, narrow pieces to use later as individual plaiting elements.

5. Sew several sections together, emphasizing the joins.

6. Stack layer upon layer of plaiting varying the outside shape of each piece.

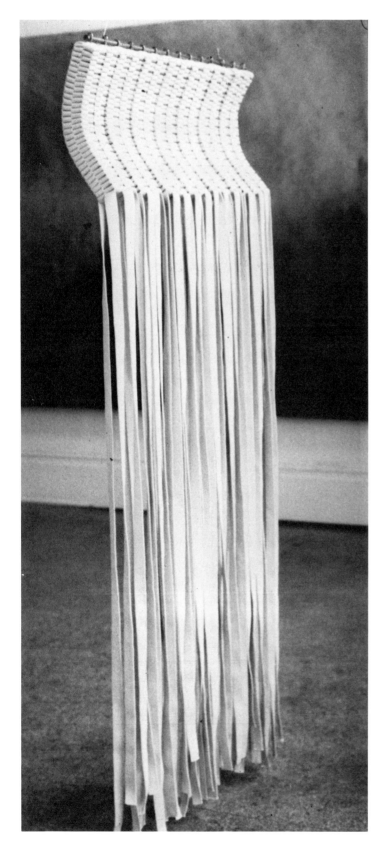

Cascading Crescent by
Thomas Siefke. 72″ x 32″
x 6″ (182.9 x 81.3 x 15.2
cm). Cotton-canvas web-
bing was used to plait this
undulating space divider.
Metal rods were woven
horizontally into the piece
to hold the individual
plaited units.

Burning Log by Ed Rossbach. This contemporary plaited sculpture features the use of silkscreened cotton and barrier-cloth elements.

Plaited basket by Ed Rossbach. The cut edges of the folded, soft elements contrast with the hard edge of the printed design in this piece. Note the supplementary curving elements which break the surface pattern in both movement and color.

SCULPTURAL PLAITING

When beginning a shaped piece with a basket start, it is important to remember that the starting place need not be the base. This limitation will tend to influence the look of every piece. There will always be a flat base on which other forms are built. In fact, the start could be a side and the piece might rest securely on rows of points.

Although many traditional pieces were containers, we are not limited by this necessity. Forms can be closed or barely open or open near the base and closed at the top. A base is not a necessary point of departure at all. Plaited pieces can move as any other art form can, from floor to ceiling to wall, etc.

Forming a plaited piece directly into the desired shape is a very exciting process which requires planning and careful attention to detail. The following list gives guidelines for your exploration:

1. Shape an irregular form by sometimes tightly working the diagonal plaiting, sometimes loosely plaiting. This could be accomplished in even bands or in small areas to give an asymmetric shape.

2. At any desired point, start making a corner and then continue plaiting. The piece will become narrower, with the started corner producing a point.

3. Making many corners on the surface can dramatically change a shape. Forming corners in rows produce lines of triangular ridges.

4. Plait over a preexisting shape or object that will be visible and important to the piece or completely hidden and serving only as a support.

5. A base started with an uneven number will produce a diamond-shaped base. Try using four vertical elements with eight horizontal elements.

6. Plait ends back into a basket with a twist to make surface patterns like the rice-grain pattern.

7. Form a shoulder by gradually overlapping strips in pairs; a neck will form when strips have been reduced by half.

8. Change elements dramatically in width to distort the shape.

9. Use both soft and stiff elements within the same piece. Start a basket base by forming only one corner. Continue plaiting around this and you will have a cone shape. Make only two corners and an envelope shape will result. By contrast, multitudes of corners can be formed at the base to give a very elaborate, exaggerated edge while the sides will still form into a cylinder.

10. Stuff a shape with a wad of unplaited elements and pull them through the surface to stick out in thick bunches or as sparse guard hairs.

FLAT OR SCULPTURAL PLAITING

Many variations can apply to both flat and sculptural plaiting. It is most interesting that both techniques work well together. The dividing line between them can be indistinct as flat and shaped areas merge and flow one from the other. Following is a list of ideas that you will probably add to as you continue working:

1. Decorate the surface with fringe, feathers, or plastic.

2. Try knotting pile onto the plaited surface.

3. Overlap strands in diagonal plaiting to leave open spaces.

4. Alternate parallel and diagonal plaiting in bands.

5. While a piece is in progress, split the strips to change the scale from a large pattern to a fine one. At a later point, reverse this and work several fine strips together as one.

Fragment-Self by Susan Jamart. 27″ x 21″ (68.6 x 53.3 cm). This self-portrait was plaited during the summer of 1974 at Haystack. The piece is cotton-canvas webbing and the photographic image was placed on the fabric with projection-speed emulsion.

6. Combine plaiting with other techniques, for example, wrapping.

7. Vary the plaited pattern from under-one, over-one to under-six, over-three, etc.

6. While plaiting, leave some strands unworked. Go back later and work with these to form an extension. Extra strips might have to be added at this point.

9. Wrap an additional strip around four contiguous plaited strips and insert it back into itself until a lump or bump is formed.

10. Combine a set of standard flat elements with one set of narrow elements such as string or yarn.

COLOR

Due to the over-under structure of the technique, any use of color other than a uniform tone will generate a fragmented, lively movement. Random color strips in a diagonal-plaited piece cross rhythmically giving areas of solid color alternating with broken colored lines. Try these uses of color:

1. *Anyam gila* can have an extra set of thinner strips of another color worked over and under every other original strip.

2. Embellish the plaited strip itself; paint it, cut small holes in it, staple it, or change the surface.

3. Plait with paired elements, and each side of the piece will be a different color.

4. Vary the color of the plaited strips in one piece.

5. Overlay has tremendous color and design possibilities. Plait additional strips to form an overlay design over an already complete piece.

6. Wrap the plaiting strips with another, narrower element before they are plaited. Leave parts of the original strip showing through.

7. As strips run out, join strips of another color.

8. Paint or draw on the surface after a piece is complete.

9. Silkscreen an image onto fabric, then cut and plait.

10. Use the printing on newspaper strips for a message.

END TREATMENTS

Historically, bases and corners are frequently reinforced. The reinforcing wood, metal, or leather and the method of attachment are often a strong part of the visual impact. Basket edges can fray easily so fragile rims often need strengthening. Following are some suggestions for end treatments:

1. Try the Hopi basket technique of lashing ends of strips over a separate rim.

2. Edges can be smooth, serrated, fringed, or a combination of these.

3. Large enclosed forms, either regular or irregular, can be plaited together to eliminate a rimlike end.

4. Consider emphasizing pins or stitches that temporarily hold the edge in place and make them permanent.

5. Reinforce the form with another material until the supporting material becomes as important visually as the plaiting.

ADDING ELEMENTS

Once a plaited piece is begun, additions are traditionally only replacement parts. Instead, the following suggestions will open up the plaited surface to a very rich flow of shape changes:

1. Plait an extension or pocket by passing several strands through the major

Room-Separation: 1973 by Lisa Rehsteiner. 88″ x 60″ x 4″ (223.5 x 152.4 x 10.2 cm). Dyed-cotton piping cord and dyed linen strips were used to plait this large room divider.

(Above) Beach Occurence of Tongues by Neda Al-Hilali. Ca. 25 yds. x 30 yds. (22.9 x 27.4 m). This environmental sculpture made of plaited paper was located on Venice Beach.

(Right) Wall relief by Neda Al-Hilali. Ca. 6 feet square (1.8 m square). Plaited and processed paper.

plaited section. Begin working with these strands while they remain attached.

2. As ends run out, overlap several in each place and gradually fan them out and work through all of them.

3. Contemporary baskets from India add additional elements at the base. The whole surface of the piece can be extended in this manner.

THE FUTURE OF PLAITING

Plaited forms and shapes, as they range from flat sheets to sharp, pointed cones, will, by their nature, enlarge and change the definition of fiber art. The smooth, complex structure and use of flat materials are both unique in textiles, while the full esthetic possibilities of the technique remain to be explored.

Only a few contemporary artists have made a serious investigation of plaiting. Among these are Ed Rossbach in California, Olga de Amaral in Colombia, and Mona Hessing in Australia. Large minimally wrapped skeins are loosely plaited in some of Sheila Hicks pieces.

Historically, plaiting has given a subtle yet distinctive beauty to household and other utilitarian implements. Now and into the future, we envision the technique used in novel ways—new lines, new forms, and new materials. Hopefully, our readers will share in this growth and make unique contributions to the evolving definition of the plaited form.

Tongues by Neda Al-Hilali. Ca. 20 feet x 20 feet by 30 feet (6 x 6 x 9 m). Suspended plaited paper.

(Left) Untitled floor sculpture by Patty Jones. 4' wide, 12' long (1.2 x 3.6 m). Plastic strips were used to create this floor sculpture. The length of the piece varies according to the amount of stretch placed on the plaiting. The piece responds to tension in much the same manner as an accordion.

(Above) Computer tape cubes by Adrian Paris. Assorted sizes to 4" (10.2 cm). Tagboard tapes from computer sheets are utilized here to form highly intricate plaited shapes.

150

SUPPLIERS LIST

We have a theory about supplies—they're where you find them. However, we also realize that both of us are natural born "junkers" and living near New York City has enabled us to come up with many new, novel sources of flat elements at very inexpensive prices. For those who prefer more traditional sources, we include the following list:

Any good fabric store
(plastic sheeting, belting, tapes, ribbons, etc.)

Baltimore Canvas Products Company
2861 West Franklin
Baltimore, Maryland 21223
(cotton canvas webbing, canvas products)

Dime stores or drugstores
(Rit and Tintex dyes, etc.)

The Mannings
R.D. 2
East Berlin, Pennsylvania 17316
(the East Coast answer to Naturalcraft, see below)

Naturalcraft
2199 Bancroft Way
Berkeley, California 94704
(the ultimate in fiber supplies)

Tandy Leather Company Stores
(all kinds of leather, tools, etc.)

Tanners' Council of America
411 Fifth Avenue
New York, New York 10016
(detailed directory of tanners and their specialities)

The Yarn Shop at Bishop Museum
Bishop Museum Grounds
Honolulu, Hawaii 96818
(Pacific craft materials, pandanus, coconut fibers, etc.)

Interwoven Rhapsodies of My Mind *by Shereen LaPlantz. 64" x 44" x 2½" (162.6 x 111.8 x 6.4 cm). Aluminum flashing was manipulated to shape in this wall piece.*

Plaited Bride by Carol Westfall. 10' x 3½' (3 x 1.1 m). Two different sizes of nylon mesh were plaited to form this sculptural wallpiece.

BIBLIOGRAPHY

BOOKS

Austin, Robert, and Ueda, Koichiro. *Bamboo*. New York and Tokyo: Walker/Weatherhill, 1970.

Barker, June. *Decorative Braiding and Weaving*. Massachusetts: Charles T. Branford Company, 1973.

Belen, Hermogenes F. *Philippine Creative Handicrafts*. Manila: C.F. David and Sons Pub., 1953

Chase, Judith Wragg. *Afro-American Art and Craft*. New York: Van Nostrand Reinhold, 1971.

Coart, E. *Vannerie et Tissage Congolais*. Bruxelles: Editions de la Rennaissance d'Occident, 1926.

Cooke, Viva, and Sampley, Julia. *Palmetto Braiding and Weaving*. Peoria: Manual Arts Press, 1947.

Den Svenska Hemslojden (Handcraft in Sweden). Stockholm: Victor Pettersons Bokindustriaktiebolog, 1951.

Dorner, Gerd. *Folk Art of Mexico*. New York: A.S. Barnes and Company, 1962.

Ficld, Clark. *The Art and the Romance of Indian Basketry*. Tulsa: Philbrook Art Center, 1964.

Goodloe, William H. *Coconut Palm Frond Weaving*. Rutland, Vermont and Tokyo: Charles E. Tuttle Company, Inc., 1972.

Harvey, Virginia I. *The Techniques of Basketry*. New York: Van Nostrand Reinhold Company, 1974.

James, George Wharton. *Indian Basketry*. California: printed privately, 1901.

Jasper, Door, J.E. *De Inlandsche Kunstnijverheid in Nederlandsch Indie. Het Vlechtwerk*. Vol. I. The Netherlands: V/H Mouton and Company, 1912.

Jefferson, Louise E. *The Decorative Arts of Africa*. New York: The Viking Press, 1973.

Kitao, Harumichi. *Formation of Bamboo*. Tokyo: Shokokuska, 1958.

Levi-Strauss, Claude. *La Pensée Sauvage*. Paris: Librairie Plon, 1962.

Lyford, Carrie A. *Iroquois Crafts*. United States Department of the Interior, Bureau of Indian Affairs, 1945.

Maes, Dr. J. *Vannerie au Lac Leopold II*, Bruxelles, 1936.

Mason, Otis T. *Indian Basketry-Studies in a Textile Art Without Machinery*. New York: Page and Company, 1904.

Meyer-Heisig, Erich. *Deutsche Volkskunst*. Munich: Prestel Verlag, 1954.

Miles, Charles. *American Indian and Eskimo Basketry*. San Francisco: Pierre Bovis, 1969.

Osborne, Lilly de Jongh. *Indian Crafts of Guatemala and El Salvador*. Oklahoma: University of Oklahoma Press, 1965.

Rossbach, Ed. *Baskets as Textile Art.* New York: Van Nostrand Reinhold Company, 1973.

Roth, Walter Edmond. *Some Technological Notes from the Pomeroon District, British Guiana.* London: Royal Anthropological Institute of Great Britain and Ireland, 1909.

Seiler-Baldinger, Annemarie. *Systematik der Textilen Techniken.* Basel: Pharos-Verlag Hansrudolf Schwabe AG, 1973.

Sourek, Karel. *Folk Art in Pictures.* London: Spring Books.

Stall, Edna Williamson. *The Story of Lauhala.* Honolulu: Paradise of the Pacific, Limited, 1953. (Available from the Bernice P. Bishop Museum, Honolulu.)

Stephens, Cleo M. *Willow Spokes and Wickerwork.* Pennsylvania: Stackpole Books, 1975.

Sugemura, Tsune, and Suzuki, Hisao. *Living Crafts of Okinawa.* New York and Tokyo: Weatherhill, 1973.

Toor, Frances. *Made in Italy.* New York: Alfred A. Knopf, 1957.

Trowell, Margaret. *African Design.* New York, Washington: Frederick A. Praeger, 1960.

———. *Tribal Crafts of Uganda.* London: Oxford University Press, 1953.

White, Mary. *More Baskets and How to Make Them.* New York: Doubleday, Page and Company, 1903.

Whiteford, Andrew Hunter. *North American Indian Arts.* New York: Golden Press, Western Publishing Company, 1970.

Willey, Gordon R. *An Introduction to American Archaeology.* Vol. I. New Jersey: Prentice-Hall, 1966.

Zechlin, Ruth. *Das Flechtbuch.* Ravensburg: Otto Maier Verlag, 1954.

PERIODICALS

Ayres, Edward M., and Duka, Luis. *Basketry Weaves in Use in the Philippines.* Manila: The Philippine Craftsman. Vol. V. No. 5. November 1916.

Bamboo. Basle: Ciba Review, 1969/3.

Barrett, S.A. *The Cayapa Indians of Ecuador.* New York: Indian Notes and Monographs, Misc. Series No. 40. Part II. Museum of the American Indian. 1925.

Belknap, William, Jr. *Twentieth Century Indians Preserve Customs of the Cliff Dwellers.* Washington, D.C.: The National Geographic. Vol. 125. No. 2. February 1964.

Bland, L.E. *A Few Notes on the "Anyam Gila" Basket Making at Tanjong Kling, Malacca.* Singapore: Royal Asiatic Society of Great Britain and Ireland Journal, Malayan Branch. No. 46. 1906.

Brigham, William T. *Mat and Basket Weaving of the Ancient Hawaiians.* Honolulu: Memoirs of the Bernice Pauahi Bishop Museum. Vol. II. No. 1. 1906.

Buhler, Dristin. *Basic Textile Techniques.* Basle: Ciba Review. No. 63. January 1948.

Chi-lu, Chen. *Basketry of the Budai Rukai.* Taiwan: Bulletin of the Department of Archeology and Anthropology. No. 11. National Taiwan University. 1958.

Douglas, Frederic H., ed. *Red-Dark-Light in Designs.* Colorado: Denver Art Museum Leaflet 114. 1951.

Fischel, Walter G. *Maori Textile Technique.* Basle: Ciba Review. No. 84. February 1951.

Fisher, Herbert D. *Filipino Hats.* Manila: The Philippine Craftsman. Vol. V. No. 5. November 1916.

Goggin, John M. *Plaited Basketry in*

the New World. Albuquerque: Southwestern Journal of Anthropology. Vol. V. 1949.

Handy, Willowdean Chatterson. Handcrafts of the Society Islands. Honolulu: Bernice P. Bishop Museum Bulletin 42. 1927.

Hiroa, Te Rangi (Peter H. Buck). Arts and Crafts of Hawaii. Honolulu: Bishop Museum Special Publication 45. 1957.

———. Maori Plaited Basketry and Plaitwork. Wellington: Royal Society of New Zealand, Transactions and Proceedings. Vol. 55. 1923.

Holme, C. The Uses of Bamboo in Japan. London: Transactions of the Japan Society of London. Vol. I. 1892.

Hornell, James. Primitive Types of Water Transport in Asia: Distributions and Origins. London: Journal of the Royal Asiatic Society of Great Britain and Ireland, 1946.

Laufer, Berthold. Chinese Baskets. Chicago: Anthropology Design Series No. 3. Field Museum of Natural History. 1925.

Lismer, Marjorie. Seneca Splint Basketry. Indian Handcrafts No. 4. U. S. Dep. of the Interior. 1941.

Mason, Otis T. Anyam Gila (Mad Weave): A Malaysian Type of Basket Work. Washington, D.C.: Proceedings United States National Museum. Vol. 36. 1909.

———. Basketry Bolo Case From Basilan Island. Washington, D.C.: Proceedings United States National Museum. Vol. 33. 1908.

———. Vocabulary of Malaysian Basketwork: A Study in the W.L. Abbot Collections. Washington, D.C.: Proceedings United States National Museum. Vol. 35. 1908.

Merwin, B.W. Basketry of the Chitimacha Indians. Philadelphia: The Museum Journal, The University Museum, University of Pennsylvania. Vol. X. 1919.

Osborne, Douglas. Solving the Riddles of Wetherill Mesa. Washington, D.C.: The National Geographic. Vol. 125. No. 2. February 1964.

Pepper, George H. The Ancient Basket Makers of Southeastern Utah. New York: American Museum of Natural History Supplement to American Museum Journal. Vol. II. No. 4. Guide Leaflet No. 6. 1902.

Phillipps, W.J. Notes on Maori Plaits. Wellington: Polynesian Society Journal. Vol. 58. 1949.

Roth, Walter Edmund. An Introductory Study of the Arts, Crafts and Customs of the Guiana Indians. Washington, D.C.: Bureau of American Ethnology, 38th Annual Report. 1916–1917.

Shelford, R. On Two Medicine Baskets from Sarawak. London: Journal of the Royal Anthropological Institute of G. B. and Ireland. Vol. 33. 1903.

Vaillant, George C. Artists and Craftsmen in Ancient Central America. New York: The American Museum of Natural History, Guide Leaflet Series No. 88. 1935.

Vogt, E. Basketry and Woven Fabrics of the European Stone and Bronze Ages. Basle: Ciba Review. No. 54. 1947.

Weltfish, Gene. Preliminary Classification of Prehistoric Southwestern Basketry. Washington, D.C.: Smithsonian Miscellaneous Collections. Vol. 87. No. 7. 1932.

Wheatley, Oliver. Japanese Ornamental Basket Work. New York: International Studio. Vol. 43. March-June 1911.

Woolley, G. E. Some Notes on Murut Basket Work and Patterns. Royal Asiatic Society, Journal of the Malayan Branch. Vol. 7. 1929.

Ripening Light by Kaye Freeman, 1973. 48" x 76" (121.9 x 193 cm). Acrylic and canvas wallpiece.

INDEX

Antique handkerchief sachet. This piece shown without the flat lid was found in New England and was used to store handkerchiefs. It is plaited at the bottom and twined on top.

Edited by Sarah Bodine
Designed by Bob Fillie
Set in 11 point Medallion by Publishers Graphics, Inc.
Printed and bound by Interstate Book Manufacturers, Inc.